# *The Art of*
# Catching &
# Cooking
# Shrimp

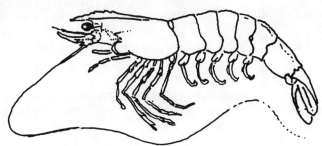

## Lynette L. Walther
### Art by Daniel G. Coston

Published and distributed by:
**William H. McCauley, Publications & Imports**
115 N. Race Street
Georgetown, DE 19947
Ph: (302) 856-6441
Fx: (302) 856-7702

Third Printing, June 1993

# *Contents*

For Kim

# Introduction

Lucky for you and me, shrimp are available all over the world. Whether it is the giant Alaskan coonstripe (prawn) shrimp or the South East Coast's Royal Red or the Indo-West Pacific shrimp or South American shrimp or the jumbo Kuruma-ebi shrimp (also wheel shrimp) of Japan or British Columbia's deep sea pink shrimp or Asia's (North and South America's as well) fresh water river shrimp or the tiny sand shrimp of the North American East Coast or the more familiar pink shrimp of the Gulf of Mexico or — well, you get the idea. The list goes on and on since there are more than 1,000 varieties of shrimp. Millions of pounds of the delectable morsels are harvested from the seas, bays, rivers and estuaries all over the world each year, making shrimp the most popular shellfish.

While shrimp are truly international favorites, in this country there are three standouts — or standbys if you prefer — of the commercial shrimping industry, the white, pink and brown shrimp as they are known by their common names. Chances are, these are the shrimp that will be served you when you dine out at your favorite restaurant. They will also be in your grocer's freezer, preboiled or in a breaded coating or among the fresh offerings at the seafood counter. These three varieties make up the majority of the shrimp sold in the United States. Most are caught in the Gulf of Mexico. Of an average annual 250 million pound catch, 200 million pounds come from the Gulf and 46 million pounds are harvested from along the southeast Atlantic coast. The remainder are from the northeast Atlantic coast.

Unlike the commercial fishing enterprises of, say, blue crabs or oysters, commercial shrimp fishing is a relatively new industry. Shrimp have no ancient, traditional boats designed for their capture as do oysters and crabs, lobsters, i.e. the sailing canoes of the Chesapeake or the old sailing lobster boats of New England. Even the earliest shrimp boats were motorized. The ancient Romans cultivated oysters, as have the Japanese for centuries, whereas oysters, crabs, scallops and lobsters graced the banquet tables in this country from its earliest time and shrimp were virtually ignored. They were considered not worth the effort nor worthy of interest; however, around 1902, an inventive Sicilian-American fisherman named Sollecito Salvador from Fernandina Beach, Florida changed that. Like most fishermen of his time, he was aware that shrimp ran in schools. Putting that knowledge together with the fishing technology of his day, he made the first step toward the beginning of the commercial shrimping industry in this country with the designing of a seine-type net drawn by a powered boat.

The next development in shrimping came some 10 years later when commercial fishermen from North Carolina originated the forerunner of the otter

and double rig travels which are popular with commercial shrimpers to this day. After seeing marine biologists use a similar net device to collect specimens, those North Carolina fishermen made the necessary changes and commercial shrimping was born. Even though the technology was established, it wasn't until the already known estuarine shrimping grounds were severely depleted after World War II, that the deep water commercial shrimping, as we know it today, began. Up until this time, shrimping was a haphazard affair, catching the annual "runs" of shrimp as they left their estuaries and rivers to head for the open ocean to spawn. The discovery of the off-shore shrimping grounds signaled the birth of large scale commercial shrimping.

For commercial shrimping, large concentrations of shrimp are necessary to offset the huge investments of boats and equipment of this labor-and energy-intensive method of harvesting seafood. Since 1950, the number of otter trawl shrimp boats fishing in the Gulf of Mexico and south Atlantic have more than doubled while the average catch per boat declined from 20,000 pounds (heads off) to half that amount. Until recently, the increasing price of shrimp offset the declining catches, but that situation seems to have begun a new and alarming change. The change is as old as history, but as new as the future itself. It is the mariculture of shrimp and it was practiced hundreds of years ago in

China (Confucius spoke glowingly of shrimp).

Until recent years, the farming of shrimp was put on the back burner, but the increasing demand for this succulent shellfish — in 1984, some 528 million pounds of shrimp were eaten in this country alone — has been supplemented by pond-grown shrimp imported from South America and Taiwan with the Philippines rushing to compete in this growing market. Lower in cost and very high in quality, these mariculture shrimp represent a real danger to the United States shrimping fleet. Unable to beat this competition, it is estimated that in 15 years, the current fleet of privately owned and corporate owned shrimping boats will shrink by half.

Although unfortunate for the already struggling commercial shrimping industry here, this situation could represent a real boon for the recreational shrimper. The numbers speak for themselves, fewer trawlers, more shrimp for individuals to catch; in that respect, the shrimping future does indeed look rosy.

Of course, all this is merely speculation, but interesting food for thought nonetheless; but even without these changes, shrimp are now everywhere. With good timing, a nominal investment in one or more simple catching devices, you can put your own freshly caught shrimp on your table. But, before heading for the water, let's get to know our quarry better. In recreational shrimping, a little knowledge of the animal we seek will go a long way towards success.

*A springtime ritual, blessing of the shrimp fleet is repeated at ports all over the South.*

# Getting Acquainted with Shrimp

Compared to other decopods — the lobster, for example, which can live in excess of 20 years, the king crab which has been known to live to the ripe old age of 25 years, or even the delectable blue crab which lives to three years, the life cycle of the shrimp is indeed short at about one year. Some rare individuals, usually females, have been found to be two years old, but one year is it for the vast majority of shrimp. Thus, shrimp are generally considered to be an annual crop and commercial and recreational shrimpers, including the bait shrimp industry, harvest them from the time they are juveniles in the estuaries until their move to the open sea for spawning.

Life moves fast for the shrimp — beginning with the hatching of eggs which occurs in the early spring for most species. About one day after spawning, which for most species of shrimp is in the open ocean, the eggs hatch. Females of some species lay up to 1,000,000 eggs. Of course, only a few will survive and reach maturity. In most species, the newly hatched crustacea are called larva and look drastically different from adult shrimp. The word "larva" comes from the Latin meaning for "mask," as the tiny shrimp are seemingly disguised from their elders. In the weeks that follow, the little shrimp will assume several "disguises" as they grow with each molt. Soon after hatching, the shrimp larva join other shrimp larva and that of other crustacea and drifting microorganisms of which, together, are called plankton — a Greek term meaning "wander." Solely dependent upon the great ocean currents the shrimp larva, as members of plankton, begin to drift. Because the larva of most shrimp require waters of low salinity in which to mature, their Odyssey begins as soon as they hatch. In addition to a half dozen changes which make the tiny animal a little larger with each change and a little more complex in structure as each state in its life quickly passes, the little shrimp is slowly drifting on the ocean currents — hopefully toward shore and an area of suitably brackish water, perhaps a tidal river or into an estuary where it will continue to develop and grow. Those that do not, will not survive. Those that do, will dwell on the bottom of their estuarine nursery.

Although it is just a theory, marine biologists believe that the tiny shrimp can somehow detect slight changes in salinity levels of the waters in which they are drifting. While these infant shrimps are not able to swim strongly enough to buck the tidal forces, they are believed to be able to swim or drift to the upper levels of waters on the incoming tides, thereby taking advantage of favorable currents which will take them into the estuaries. Conversely, when the outgoing tides, with their lowered salinity, begin, the tiny shrimp settle down to the bottom, waiting there until the tide changes. This process seems to work in reverse with the mature shrimp as they make their way back to the open ocean — rising to the top on the outgoing tides to let those currents take them away from their estuaries. And, then during the incoming tide, they settle down to the bottom, not fighting the current. This, of course, is mainly speculation on the part of scientists, but this knowledge can be put to use by recreational shrimpers — taking the opportunity of outgoing tides which seem to bring the creatures up from their burrows in the bottom, creating vast migrations of adult shrimp in the late summer and early fall.

By the time summer has arrived, the juvenile shrimp look exactly like their parents, only smaller. Next, these small shrimp move into the deeper waters of the bays, rivers and estuaries to mature until the arrival of cool weather, which will slow their growth and send them to the open ocean for deeper, warmer waters where they will follow the path of their parents and spawn in the spring. A year passes and many of the new generation of shrimp reach a size of five inches. Those adults that aren't caught in the trawl nets of the offshore shrimp boats are destined to die soon after mating and spawning.

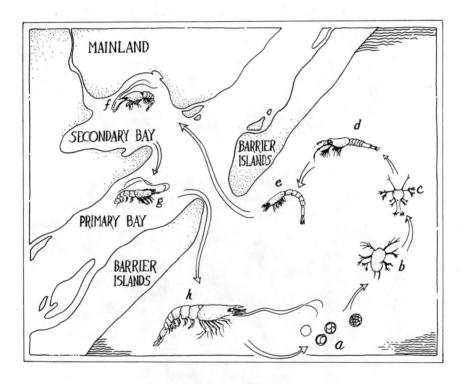

*Life Cycle of shrimp*

In many areas of the Southern coastal waters, shrimping seasons are geared to this life cycle, insuring replenishment of the next generation of shrimp. Knowing the shrimp's life cycle and timetable, we can take advantage of the fact this these gregarious decapods predictably gather at the end of the summer to travel from their inland or estuarine nurseries, out to sea. Historically, these great migrations have meant shrimping bonanzas for recreational shrimpers.

# *Varieties*

Recreational shrimpers who live on the Atlantic coast have a decided advantage over their neighbors on the Pacific coast. Ample food, estuarine environments and the warm waters of the Gulf Stream and the Gulf of Mexico provide perfect growing conditions for the Atlantic-based shrimp. The colder waters of the Pacific mean the shrimp grow more slowly and therefore are not as prevalent as in the southeast Atlantic. Nonetheless, there are plenty of shrimp on both coasts to satisfy all.

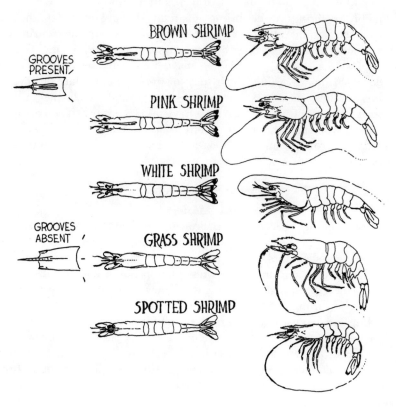

GROOVES PRESENT

BROWN SHRIMP

PINK SHRIMP

WHITE SHRIMP

GROOVES ABSENT

GRASS SHRIMP

SPOTTED SHRIMP

As I have already mentioned, the three commercially important white shrimp (Penaeus Litopenaeus setiferus); brown shrimp (Penaeus Melicertus aztecus aztecus); and pink shrimp (Penaeus (Melicterus) duorarum duorarum) are found on the Atlantic and Gulf of Mexico coasts. Here is the lowdown on all three:

### Atlantic Shrimp

Often nearly transparent, white shrimp, may have a bluish cast to their bodies with a darker blue on their tailfins and swimmerets and a purplish blotch near the end of the tail. In some areas, the white shrimp are called the "green shrimp" because of a greenish color they may acquire under certain circumstances. Still other examples of white shrimp can display a dark band of specks along the rear margin of the carapace. In these white shrimp, the body sides have an almost pink color with reddish swimmerets and legs.

Confused? This may help. A distinguishing characteristic of all white shrimp is their long antennae. They are nearly twice as long as the body. There is also a long spike or rostrum found on the white shrimp's head. Grab this fellow the wrong way and it could cause a painful wound. I've seen times when they have landed spike down, imbedding the spike in the dock when they are shaken from a cast net. The spike is not an aggressive weapon, but can cause pain if carelessly handled.

Mature white shrimp are about five inches in length or more. Unlike the pink and brown shrimp, white shrimp apparently do not burrow into the bottom during the day, for often the greatest catches of these are made during the daylight hours. While traveling the Intracoastal Waterway in the Halifax River at Daytona Beach, Florida, we have frequently seen summertime recreational shrimpers casting nets by day for the abundant white shrimp. So numerous are these shrimpers, anchored in and around the channel in their small boats, that they frequently create a navigational hazard. If you are after white shrimp, you can fish for it from Fire Island to Florida, where it can be found along the Atlantic and Gulf Coasts, occurring in heavy concentrations along the Georgia and North Florida Coasts.

### Brown Shrimp

The brown shrimp, because of its brownish coloration, sometimes has a yellow or orange tint, deeper on its legs and tailfin. Speckled sides are common on younger shrimp of this variety which averages about four inches in length. Like the pink shrimp, the brown shrimp spends its days in sub-aquatic "burrows," emerging at night — a time when they are often fished with trawls by commercial shrimpers. Initially more difficult to market than white and pink shrimp, an intensive government/shrimping industry marketing campaign a few years ago convinced the shellfish loving public that the browns are every bit as tasty as white and pink shrimp. The brown shrimp now ranks first in numbers of pounds landed commercially. Brown shrimp are found from Martha's Vineyard to the Florida Keys and all around the Gulf Coast to the Yucatan.

## Pink Shrimp

While all shrimp are delicious, the pink shrimp are the loveliest of the lot. A delicate shell pink, these shrimp often have a beauty spot of sorts, a purplish or reddish spot on each side where the third and fourth abdominal somites meet. In some areas, these shrimp, which average five inches in length and are often longer, are called the pink-spotted or spotted shrimp. In other areas, especially where the pink shrimp are taken in deeper waters, they are called red shrimp because of their intensified color. Commercial trawl fishing for the pink shrimp is the most recent of the three varieties sought (white, brown and pink), beginning around 1950. This variety is found in great concentrations in deeper waters for trawl fishing at depths of 11 to 20 fathoms. The pink shrimp prefer the Southern waters and can be found southward from the Chesapeake Bay to the Florida Keys and along the Gulf of Mexico coast to Mexico. Greatest concentrations of these shrimp are found in the waters surrounding the Dry Tortugas in the Gulf of Mexico. Like the brown shrimp, the pink shrimp spend their days in burrows and are fished at night when they leave their burrows to feed.

## Other Shrimp on Atlantic Coast

Other shrimp found along the Atlantic Coast are the intertidal prawn *(Palaemonetes vulgaris)*, a translucent shrimp with brown spots. These shrimp can grow to five inches in length and are frequently found in eelgrass beds in tidal waters from New Hampshire south to Florida.

\* \* \*

Another small, translucent shrimp often found in eelgrass beds is the *Hippolyte (Virbius) zastericola,* but its range only extends from Massachusetts to New Jersey. Like the intertidal prawn, these shrimp are frequently referred to as "grass shrimp."

\* \* \*

The sand shrimp *(Crangon septemspinosus)* are the most commonly found shrimp of the upper Atlantic Coast, ranging from the far north of Labrador to North Carolina. About three inches long, these grayish, translucent shrimp are distinguished by star-shaped dark spots on their bodies. Offshore sand bars and onshore sand flats are the best places to find these shrimp.

## Pacific Coast Shrimp

Pacific Coast shrimp are some of the most colorful, with the costume prize going to the coon-striped shrimp which wears various patterns, depending on their locale. Most commonly, they are dressed in green and brown stripes with a characteristic feature of a pair of pincers topping their long slender second pair of legs. These, like most shrimp, are nocturnal and found in bays and estuaries. An old automobile tire, fashioned into a cozy cave of a trap is one favorite method of taking these shrimp in the summer months, but more on that in the next chapter. These shrimp are frequently found in Alaska and range south to upper California.

### Black-Tailed Shrimp

The black tailed shrimp *(crago nigricanda)* are abundant along the entire Pacific Coast from Alaska to Baja California. They are fished commercially there, going from shallow waters in the summer to deeper offshore waters during the winter months. Attaining a length of about five inches, the black-tailed shrimp are speckled with salt and pepper markings, even on their legs and antennae.

Basically, these are the shrimp we will be going for, though there are others available in various areas. They are all tasty and not as difficult to catch as you might think. Now that we know what we are looking for, it's time to move on to the serious business, make that "fun business," of catching shrimp.

# *Catching Shrimp*

One night while motoring along the Intracoastal Waterway in our sailboat, Patience, just north of Florida's Mosquito Lagoon, we happened upon an almost magical scene. It was as if there were a lighted corridor running along the channel. Our sentries were dozens and dozens of small boats with bright lights aimed at the glassy surface of the water. The vision spread before us for miles. Their occupants were shrimping. The time was early June and earlier that day we had seen shrimpers along the Halifax River near Daytona Beach, casting their nets for shrimp. The shrimpers there fished in the light of day, but here, a little farther south by about 30 miles at the entrance to Mosquito Lagoon, the shrimping was done at night, as it is done where I live on the St. Johns River.

Well, almost as it is done on the St. Johns. There was no chumming involved in this operation and the shrimpers didn't use cast nets. Instead, they had huge long-handled dip nets with mouths of about two feet in diameter. The nets themselves were five feet or more long. As the shrimp were lured into the circles of light, the shrimpers would dip the shrimp up, shaking them down to the "toes" of the nets which dangled in the water. The shrimp stayed there until the shrimper was ready to empty the net. The eerie scene was like a silent ceremony. No one made a sound. We motored along with a hushed "pufft-pufft" of our diesel engine as the large, filmy nets dipped to one side and then the other, as if in salute to our passing. The drops of water coming off the nets looked like showers of diamonds in the brilliant lights. It was magical.

Indeed, there will always be something magical about catching shrimp for me. Perhaps it is because our shrimping often is done under the cover of darkness, or perhaps it is just because it is so easy to catch something so special, something which remains, even now, a bit mysterious to us all.

The first time I realized what "sitting ducks" shrimp were, was while cruising in the Bahamas.

It was a calm and moonless night. Bob, my husband and our daughter, Kim, and I were anchored on the lea shore of Gun Cay. We were settling down for some sleep before the next day's long trip across the Grand Bahama Bank. Our little boat would be accompanied on the long trip by three other sailboats. But that evening, noises from the other boats aroused our attention and curiosity and we went topside to see what was going on. Once on deck we were amazed by a spectacle that had not been equalled before or since on our many trips to the islands. The glassy calm and dark water writhed with tiny bursts of neon-green lights — as far as the eye could see. We joined the crews of the other sailboats with "oohs and aahs" as the light show continued. A lantern held close to the surface of the night-blackened water did not reveal the source of the bursts of color, but the small translucent shapes and red eyes of shrimps soon gathered in the light. Attracted by the bright light of the lantern, like moths to a flame, the shrimp, in turn, attracted fish: predators. A quick hand with a dip net could have captured the ingredients of a court bouillon.

While in the Bahamas, the prevalent shrimp never seemed much of a temptation, what with all the fresh crawfish (lobster) so handy. Even the sweet and chewy conch seemed a better catch, being so plentiful, slow and easy to catch. But once we returned to our home port in time to escape the hurricane season in the safety of Florida's St. Johns River, we found that shrimp were causing quite a stir on the St. Johns as they made their yearly run on the river — heading out to sea to spawn.

Euell Gibbons, one of the greatest stalkers of wild foods, both animal and vegetable, and author of the classic *Stalking the Blue-Eyed Scallop,* stated in that book, "The trouble is I have never figured a way to catch my own supply of shrimp..." This is a complete mystery to me, because shrimp are possibly one of the easiest shellfish to catch.

I don't want to oversimplify the situation by saying that shrimping is like fishing in a barrel, but that's just about the way it is. The key to this statement is, of course, a pair of variables: timing and location. When the shrimp are running, if you are in the right place at the right time, it is almost difficult not to catch them. Shrimp follow a fast-ticking biological timeclock. They spend the late spring and early summer in relative isolation, feeding on aquatic plants and animal matter and organic debris and often spend their days in sub-aquatic burrows. Come late summer most mature shrimp will join others of their kind, forming great schools of thousands and thousands of shrimp. These schools will frequently travel by night, often being the most active on the ebb tide of a full moon as they move toward the sea to spawn the coming generation.

Temperature is probably the most important factor in determining shrimp populations in any given year. This will influence survival rates and growth, as well as migration times. Shrimp grow rapidly during the warmer months, but their growth slows or often stops completely during winter months. Extremely cold winters in the South, as experienced in the winters of 1977 and 1978 then again in 1983 and 1984, took their toll on shrimp populations. Other environmental factors, salinity, fluctuations of rainfall, river discharges and ocean currents all play important roles in determining sizes of shrimp populations each year. For example, heavy rainfalls can result in mass inshore-offshore movements of shrimp populations, due to lowered inland salinity levels.

Habitat preferences can be noted in the white, pink and brown shrimp. Brown and pink shrimp prefer a higher salinity, with their inshore habitats characterized by a bottom of a mixture of shell, sand and mud, while the white shrimp generally prefer a low salinity of brackish, or almost fresh water. They also thrive where the soft bottoms are rich in detritus and other nutrients — as found in the St. Johns River where I do my shrimping. Most active of the species, the white shrimp are also the least hardy, being more susceptible to environmental fluctuations like low temperatures and differences in salinity. Shrimp frequently migrate long distances for their annual spawning migrations, but also in search for food.

Frequently found in upper reaches of sounds and bays, as well as in many rivers and tidal creeks, the young shrimp grow rapidly on diets of detritus, small marine worms, tiny crabs, other small shellfish and other shrimp as well. Shrimp usually crawl along the bottom with their walking legs when feeding and have been observed feeding on very small fish and squid which they attack. They are also scavengers like their cousins, the blue crabs.

Old timers tell of how, on moonlit Southern August nights, recreational shrimpers of 30, 40 or 50 years ago, used kerosene lanterns to illuminate the surface of the water to attract shrimp. In some areas, shrimpers of yesteryear burned "lighter knots," resinous pine knots, in wire baskets suspended over the water to cast a glow of light. These baskets were attached to long poles extended outover the water from anchored boats or from "shrimp stands."

## SHRIMP STAND

Remains of these old shrimp stands can be found in many areas. They appear to be docks built out over the water with no connection to the shore. The shrimpers rowed out to the stands, set up their lights, put out their chum and began the series of casting their nets out over the spheres of light. Even today the monofilament cast net and kerosene lantern are still two of the most popular pieces of equipment used by recreational shrimpers. Many say that a flickering light like that of a lantern, as opposed to that of an electrical light, is more attractive to the shrimp. But the cast net is by far not the only method that can be used to catch shrimp. With catching methods and equipment often varying from area to area, these can include the whole spectrum from a simple dip net to a variety of specialized pot-style shrimp traps to sophisticated recreational trawling outfits.

Before you set out in search of shrimp — take time to check the legalities of the sport in your area. Is a license required? In most cases you won't need one if you are using a cast net, but it is likely you will if you plan to trap shrimp with a shrimp trap or seine them in a trawl net. What are the legal waters in your area? Know the boundaries. Is there a legal shrimping season? This is strictly enforced in some areas and non-existent in others. Are there size and quantity limits? What about gear and gear size restrictions? In my state, shrimp traps can be no longer than 36-inches long by 24-inches wide by 12-inches high and cannot have any external wings or wires. An individual cannot work more than four traps at any time. Also shrimp traps cannot be left unattended and must have the owner's name and address affixed to them. Know the laws where you plan to shrimp, get your equipment ready and let's go!

# *Dip Nets*

One of the simplest methods of recreational shrimping is with a light and a dip net. A fine mesh, no larger than 3/8 inch, is necessary to keep the shrimp from escaping through the mesh. On warm summer evenings in South Florida, shrimpers line the ocean piers. Since these piers are sometimes 20 to 30 feet from the surface of the sea, shrimpers use dip nets with extension handles. They lower their kerosene lanterns by ropes to just above the water's surface and soon the lights begin to attract the shrimp. What comes next is the closest thing to fishing in a barrel that I know of, since all the shrimper has to do is lower the long-handled net and dip up the shrimp from the pools of light. That's all there is to it! Several times each summer, shrimp will "run," often on the full of the moon, on the outgoing tide and this will bring out the local shrimpers in force.

## DIP NET

In other areas, like Mosquito Lagoon, which I've already described, the nets are of another design, but are dip nets nonetheless. There, dip nets have handles of about six feet in length, but it is the nets themselves that are different. Those nets are almost as long as their handles, being about one and one half to two feet in diameter at the hoop. From there, the nets taper slowly, making them long and cone-shaped and are called butterfly or wing nets. The Mosquito Lagoon shrimpers can dip for several shrimp, shaking them down to the "toe" of the net as they catch more. This keeps the shrimp alive since they are still in their waters for a little while, but since shrimp deteriorate rapidly after being taken from the water, the shrimpers soon relegate their catch to a cooler of ice. A bucket or cooler of ice is the best place to keep the catch as you while away the night in this pleasant pastime.

If you've never shrimped before, you may be in for a bit of a surprise, but not exactly an unexpected one. The lights, to which the shrimp are so attracted, will no doubt invite various insects as well. Be prepared for mosquitos and biting gnats. As one veteran recreational shrimper wryly put it, "There's nobody that suffers like the sportsman." But never has such suffering been so worth it.

As soon as possible, shrimp should be de-headed. If this is done within a couple hours after they are caught, the sandy black vein which runs along the shrimp's back, will simply pull out as the head is removed. Holding the shrimp in the left hand, with the underside (legs) facing you, use your right thumb and index finger to grasp the head where it joins the body. Gently pry the head back, breaking it away from the body and gently continue to pull as the sand vein slides through the shrimp's body.

Unless you are ready to cook the shrimp, there is no need to worry about peeling it at this point. In fact it is always preferable to cook and/or freeze the shrimp with its shell on, but we'll discuss this in more detail in the chapter on preparation.

My friend and publisher, Robert H. Robinson, who lives in Delaware, a state which he claims does not have a single shrimp boat, has no problem obtaining fresh shrimp from the salt water marshes near his home. He nets his own. They're small, he admits, about two inches long including the head, but they are plentiful. He uses a long handled dip net with a fine mesh and walking briskly alongside a shallow pond or creek cutting through the salt water marsh, runs the net in the water, letting it brush against the grass. Sometimes he nets as much as a cup of shrimplets with one sweep.

High tide is best, he says, but even if you want some during low tide, just dip the net in the mud, shake it in the water to free some of the mud and then dump — what he describes as "gook" — on the ground and pick out the shrimp. These shrimp may be difficult to spot since they are nearly transparent and have a tendency, as do most shrimp, to hop around like giant fleas. "But after a while," he says, "your eyes become trained to seeing them."

Many people call these shrimp, grass shrimp, but they are actually shore shrimp, Palaimonetes species, which range from Cape Cod to the Gulf of Mexico and can be found in both freshwater parts of tidal rivers and estuarine ponds and creeks. They are one of the most common shrimp and many people use them as bait. But they are delicious, says Robinson, who has tried recipe after recipe.

As soon as he catches them, he puts them on ice and he keeps them chilled until they are ready to be washed and cooked or frozen. The little shrimps can easily be frozen in a container with water. (For more information on freezing shrimp, see section on preparation).

Robinson says he prefers to boil the shrimplets for a minute before freezing them, since once the shrimp are pink, they are more defined and don't appear like a gray mass. Also, after they are cooked, it is easier to pick out any foreign matter.

He says you have to approach these shrimp with the idea that they are going to be eaten whole — heads and all. It's because these shrimp don't grow large that they actually remain tender, because their shells do not become hard. Still there is some size difference in these shrimp and the large ones — two inches and over — he fries in a batter as one would fry clam cakes.

# Cast Netting

A bit more strenuous than dip-netting, the use of a cast net for catching shrimp is probably one of the most widely used and most popular methods. Again, the cast net method of shrimping is usually done at night with kerosene or electric lights from docks or from small boats anchored in about four to eight feet of water. White shrimp run in Florida's Halifax River near Daytona Beach as early as June and daytime shrimping is popular there. There are many others areas where this is the case as well. White shrimp represent one of the few species which can be caught during daylight hours since they do not spend their days in subaquatic burrows as do the brown and pink shrimp.

In some areas complete darkness and stealth are the keys to cast netting success. Shrimpers stake out "plots," chum them, leave them and quitely return after dark — preferably in a wooden boat with muffled oars. They cast just once on each plot and are sometimes rewarded with 10 to 20 pounds on that one cast. Then they silently move on to their next plot, maybe revisiting each plot once more again that night. No lights and no noise are essential in some areas while plenty of light — from lamps or kerosene lanterns, is necessary in others.

The cast nets, which frequently come in four-five- and six-foot — and even larger diameters — are usually sold as "bait" nets with a mesh of no larger than ⅜ inch. This results in a mesh size small enought to trap shrimp. Whether you choose a nylon or monofilament net is purely a matter of personal preference. The monofilament is often less costly and is the most popular, perhaps for this reason, but it is more prone to damage. Check your net frequently for broken mesh. Oftentimes this is the main reason the shrimp seem to "stop running." They haven't left the area, they are just leaving your net through the gaps.

Cast nets are especially effective when used in tidal creeks on ebb tides where the shrimp frequently congregate at the mouths of small tributaries and sloughs along the shoreline, adjacent to the channel. The nets are thrown or "cast" in such a manner that they open to a circle and fall flat on the water when fully open. After the weighted edges of the net have settled to the bottom, the hand cord is drawn, pulling the tuck lines into the center. This forms a net "bag" which hold the shrimp.

The flatter and smoother the bottom on which you are casting, the larger diameter cast net you may use. In some areas on the Gulf of Mexico, where there are large expanses of shallow water with few obstructions, the recreational shrimpers cast nets of up to 20 feet in diameter. Cast nets vary in design as well as in diameter, one variation being the "Spanish" net which incorporates short tucks at the bottom of the net.

A relatively simple maneuver, nonetheless casting the net does take some practice. Everyone has heard the jokes about the uncoordinated cast netter who lost his false teeth as the net jerked them from his mouth. Whether you fear losing your teeth or just get tired of putting that wet, fishy net back in your mouth, one veteran cast netter (of the latter school) Woody Lee of Florida, offered this trick. He devised a simple neck clip that eliminates the need to grip the net in the teeth. His device requires a circle of cord, just large enough to slip over the head. A strong spring-clip clothes pin is strung on the cord by two holes drilled in the ends of the pin. Clip the clothes pin on the net and you'll find it holds it just enough and then lets it loose when it's thrown. But the inventor cautions that the cord you select should have "absolutely no stretch to it," or else it will snap back when the net releases, giving the cast netter an upleasant jab in the throat. He suggests sash cord or card from Venetian blinds.

For many cast-net shrimpers, their success is often credited to chumming. Chum recipes are frequently closely-guarded secrets, but in reality, one chum is pretty much the same as the next. Try mixing about one third rock salt and two thirds inexpensive dry dog food or scratch feed or fish meal. Blind this mixture with a combination of warm water and melted bacon grease. You can add a small amout of corn meal and fish meal, trying what seems to work best for conditions where you shrimp. For an evening's shrimping you'll need a couple buckets of chum, tossing some out periodically around the perimeters of the circles of light cast by your lanterns or electric lights. Re-chum whenever your net casts' catch diminish. Depending upon how the tides run on your shrimping grounds, this will be about every 15 to 30 minutes. Some shrimpers like to hand pack "meatballs" of their chum mixture which will sink to the bottom, rather than drift with the tides, which a looser chum tends to do. Rather that add water to your chum combination, try canned dog food or cat food which will result in a stiffer mixture.

Another method of chumming, which is gaining favor, is the cat-food can. Simply pierce large cans of the most inexpensive cat food you can find. Use an ice pick or punch-type can opener. Toss a few of these cans where you plan to shrimp and the cat food will be slowly releases as the evening wears on. It is a good idea to tie a string to each so they can be retrieve d and properly discarded when you're through shrimping.

If you are working from a wooden dock, you'll need to "cover" the boards with burlap or an old sheet or something similar that will let the water run through but keep the shrimp from slipping between the boards. You can dump your cast net on this surface. Cast netting is a congenial sport, best done in teams — one person throwing the net with a partner working the dock to pick up the just-caught shrimp and place them on ice. It's a good idea to use a lidded container, ice chest or covered bucket, because the shrimp can jump quite high and if left in an uncovered bucket, can easily make good their escape.

I am tempted to suggest that the person picking up the shrimp from the dock wear work gloves, because of the sharp head and tail spines on some shrimp. These tend to "shred" the fingers after a couple hours of this duty. It's wet work and the hands stay wet, softening the skin and making it even more vulnerable. Cotton gloves would soon soak through and rubber gloves would soon become full of holes. On the other hand, those heavy-duty rubberized gloves the commercial fishermen wear, would protect the hands but they wouldn't allow enough digital dexterity to pick up the flipping and jumpy shrimp. I'm not sure what the answer to this problem is, but all I can say is that shrimpin season usually isn't long. It may wreck your hands, but it is worth it to be able to squirrel away 50 to 60 pounds of fresh shrimp in the freezer. Besides, yhour fingers will heal long before your stash of shrimp is just a sweet memory.

Because throwing the cast net is strenuous, it's a good idea for the partners to switch off jobs from time to time. Some shrimpers like to dump their nets into a large wash tub which will contain their shrimp, but I find this method is not as efficient as a cloth on the dock, since the bucket also holds sticks, water and other debris and frequently has to be emptied — wasting precious shrimping time! Cast net shrimping is wet work too, not to mention dirty since your cast net will bring up mud and other debris along with the shrimp. Wear waterproof boots and old clothes.

Throwing a cast net is an art and an acquired skill, but is not too difficult for most to learn. It's also excellent exercise.

The information for throwing a cast net is from "A Recreational Guide to Oystering, Clamming, Shrimping and Crabbing in South Carolina." It is an excellent publication, printed by the South Carolina Wildlife and Marine Resources Department. The publication states the best method for learning, other than practice, is to find an old salt who is experienced and have him (or her!) show you how to cast a net. However, if no teacher is available, the illustrations and captions should suffice.

1. The following directions are for right handed persons. Place the end loop over the right hand, coil the line lasso-like around the right hand and pick up the neck with the left hand.

2. Grasp the net with the right hand approximately one-third of the way down the net and let the neck fall free.

3. Using the free hand (left hand), place one net lead in your mouth and then reach down the lead line and hold another lead at arm's length.

4. Keeping both arms straight, swing the net to the rear and then, with a swirling motion, bring the net rapidly forward opening both your left hand and mouth at the same time.

5. As the net is released with the right hand, a backward tug on the hand line and a high trajectory insure that the net will spread equally in a full circle. The caster's right arm should be fully extended and parallel to the net perimeter.

# Shrimp Traps

A relative newcomer to the sport of recreational shrimping is the shrimp trap, but it is gaining in popularity. Diversity is the catchword here with these, which are often homemade, affairs running the gamut of a converted automobile tire shrimp trap to commercially constructed models, some of which trap to commercially constructed models, some of which resemble crab pots. These traps are usually used at night, when most shrimp are active and are either feeding or migrating. My favorite model is a collapsible, commercially-made shrimp pot made of black nylon mesh on a heavy galvanized ring frame. It flattens for off-season storage and when not in use, can be hung by a hook.

*It's hard to believe that these diverse traps are all used for the same purpose — to catch shrimp. These are but a few of the shrimp traps to be found around the country. They are, clockwise from the top: a tire trap which is used at night in Alaska, a box-type shrimp trap from the Friendship Trap Co. of Maine, Gino Litrico's "Trigger Net©" and a folding nylon mesh trap from Marine Warehouse.*

One of the most interesting shrimp traps around is a recent invention by Fernandina Beach, Fla., fishing equipment researcher, Gino Litrico. A sort of an "underwater cast net," the two-piece trap is adjustable and can be used to catch other shellfish, like lobsters or crabs. He calls the recently patented trap, a "passive system, because if it is abandoned it will not continue to kill. It is either fully open or fully closed. It is a more benign method for capturing creatures."

Shrimp traps are more suited for use on an uneven or rocky or oyster shell bottom than a cast net is, because of the possible damage to the cast net on such surfaces. Most of the commercially constructed shrimp traps do not have bait wells and this is because the bait needed for shrimp must be very fine and would quickly wash or sift through most meshes durable enough to install in such traps. If they had bait wells fine enough to hold the necessary bait, then there would difficulty in cleaning them completely. For this reason, you'll need to sew a bait "sock" or bait bag, or just use an old sock or (here's yet another use for those discarded pantyhose) use a piece of pantyhose to hold your chum-type bait or fish meal and rock salt — whatever you choose to use. Most important, don't forget to check your trap frequently. Most traps will catch just as many shrimp in five minutes, as they will in 25 minutes. Many of the commercially made traps have rather large opening and these will allow entrance to the traps by fish, crabs or eels. Unless you plan to feed these free loaders a meal of freshly-caught shrimp check your traps every five or ten minutes.

Long-line fishermen use a technique when fishing for swordfish and the same ploy could work for your shrimp traps. Those deep-sea fishermen utilize the Cyalume © Lightsticks to lure fish to their lines. The same principle is used to lure shrimp into an area with lanterns, but these little lights can be used UNDER the water to help lure the shrimp into your traps. This may not work in all areas, at all times, but try setting one baited trap with one or two of these lightsticks inside. See if it attracts more shrimp than the other traps — it should — and then you can add the lightsticks to your other traps.

Where I live, there are size limitations on shrimp traps. Traps can be no larger than 36 inches long by 24 inches wide by 12 inches high and no individual can operate more than four traps. Also, shrimp traps cannot be left unattended and the owner must have his name and address on each trap. However, there is no license required for these recreational shrimp traps, no limit on catches and no closed season here. But these factors can, and often do, vary from area to area and you should always check with your local marine patrol and fish and game commission so you will know the rules and regulations associated with the use of shrimp traps in your area.

# *Seine Netting Shrimp*

I have a friend Jim White who did college research work on an island off the coast of Georgia. Being in the middle of one of the prime shrimping areas, and being totally isolated (the island was accessible only by boat) leisure time for my friend and his associates often was spent on such pursuits as shrimping. A seine net, which was frequently used by researchers for collecting marine speciment, was their method of catching great feasts of shrimp which were often cooked on the spot. He claims no shrimp have yet to compare to those on those legendary picnics.

If you plan to try shrimping with a seine net, first check restrictions and local laws governing its use. Areas of known shrimp runs are the best candidates for this method, which will require two or more people to draw the seine net. I've seen ambitious shrimp seiners who constructed a sort of lighted corridor in chest-high water to be fished at night. The corridor was lined with poles, each of which was topped with an electrical light. It looked like an electricution just waiting to happen, but the shrimpers didn't seem to notice the danger. The outfit had potential, but I'd use kerosene lights for safety. The shrimpers walked along slowly, pulling their net. I couldn't tell if any chum was used, but it may not have been since the lighted corridor was quite long, maybe 200 feet long or longer. Seining should be a good method for catching the sand shrimp or any of the small varieties found in the eel grass.

Traditional seine nets are rectangular and are often made of nylon or monofilament line webbing. A lead line runs along the bottom of the seine and a cork line runs along the top. Some seines, especially designed for shrimping, have bags or pockets into which shrimp are herded. Seining for shrimp is often done in shallow water near the shore and during daylight hours.

In many areas no license is required to seine, but there are frequently size restrictions. In some states seine nets must be no longer than 40 feet or cannot block more than one half of a creek. Mesh size must not be smaller than one-half inch square mesh nylon or 9/16-inch square mesh of cotton. Check local regulations regarding licensing and seasonal limits on seine netting. In some areas where fresh water fish may be accidentally trapped in the net, it is illegal to keep such fish and they must be released unharmed.

# Drop Nets

One of the most popular spots for recreational shrimping is from bridges. Not only are bridges easily accessible for the shrimper, but the bodies of water they span are typically prime locations for shrimp migrations. Passes, entrances to sloughs, narrow spots in tidal rivers — where bridges cross bodies of water—are frequently where the great migrations of shrimp must pass. A marine patrol officer told me of a popular bridge where, during shrimping season, recreational shrimpers have nearly come to blows over standing space. The drop net is a good choice for bridge shrimping. These "hoops" are usually about three to four-feet in diameter and have a cone-shaped net of ¼- to ¾-inch mesh. A bridle is attached to the frame and a main line to the bridle. By this main line the baited net is lowered into the water. Popular baits are cut fish, canned dog or cat food. You can try punching holes in the can with a can opener to slowly release the bait. In many areas there is no license requirement, gear restriction nor season for drop netting.

# Recreational Trawling

Without a doubt sport shrimp trawling is the most costly of all the methods so far described, but it is also the most productive and for the fisherman who already owns a power boat, the investment is not prohibitive. Many net shops or commerical fishing supply houses sell such outfits. These long, often funnel-shaped nets, are dependent on the use of otter doors, so that the mouth of the net remains open as it is drawn through the water.

THE OTTER TRAWL

Commercially, shrimp are caught by this method — in nets drawn by trawlers ranging in length from 20 to 85 feet, usually powered by diesel engines capable of developing up to 250 horsepower. For the recreational shrimper this kind of power is not necessary, but attempting to pull or tow nets with outboard engines too small for the job or using improper gear will result in very small or no catches at all. The North Carolina Sea Grant program conducted a lengthy study of recreational shrimping and that study provided a series of guidelines for both commercial and recreational shrimpers. The study found that there are basically three popular shrimp net or trawl designs — the flat net (a sort of open box with flat sides which is drawn along the bottom), the balloon net (which fishes the bottom and the water column 10 to 15 feet above the bottom) and the semi-balloon net which is a kind of a cross between the flat and the balloon nets and is the most popular of the three designs. It opens wider than the other two nets and fishes higher that the flat net, but not as high as the balloon net. Each of these nets has different flotation requirements and numbers of corks.

## DOUBLE-RIG TRAWLING

The Sea Grant study also came up with recommended net size to that of horsepower to produce the greatest catches at the lowest fuel costs. And that study showed that for motor sizes of 25 to 50 horsepower the maximum recommended net sizes are 12 to 16 feet; for 50 to 75 hp. net sizes are 12 to 20 feet; for 85 to 125 hp. net sizes are 12 to 25 feet; and for 135 to 200 hp. net sizes are 12 to 32 feet. For example, a 5½-hp outboard on a small boat can easily pull a 10-foot trawl. For nets of 25 feet or longer it is suggested a mast, a winch or a block and tackle be installed due to the great weight involved. A 25-foot shrimp net can quickly take on several hundred pounds of weight. Recreational shrimpers usually tow their nets for 30 minutes to one hour at a time. This prevents excessive weight buildup in the net. A bonus for the shrimper in the case of trawling can often be a "mixed bag" catch of seafood which can include along with the shrimp — snapper, flounder, conch and perhaps whelks.

However, there are limitations and requirements governing this type of shrimping, these usually including licenses for bait-shrimp trawling and sport fishing licenses; specific gear size limitations and restrictions; legal waters and seasons governing shrimping; and limits as to the quantities of catch and size of shrimp caught.

It is suggested that trawl shrimpers try several short trawls in different locations so that larger numbers of "under count" (smaller that legal size shrimp) are not caught. Although these shrimps can be released, once caught they will not survive. These small shrimps are often concentrated in secondary bays.

The most complicated of all shrimping methods discussed here, trawling requires sophisticated and more costly gear than any other shrimping technique. Rigging and rigging adjustments are where we must begin long before setting out upon the water.

New trawl nets do not necessarily come with otter boards or "doors". These doors regulate the horizontal spread of the net by building water pressure as the boat moves forward. The smaller doors used by recreational shrimpers are built with ¾-inch marine plywood and ¼-inch irons. Most recreational shrimpers purchase their net ready to tow, but may have to construct their own doors or otter boards. Because recreational shrimpers tow their nets for shorter lengths of time that the larger commercial trawlers, they usually reduce door widths and lengths by one-third. For the 30-minute to one-hour tows used by recreational shrimpers, use this table to calculate door to net ratios for altering commercial shrimping doors or for construction of your own:

| Door width | Door length | Net size |
|------------|-------------|----------|
| 16 inches | 2 feet 8 inches | 20 feet |
| 17 inches | 3 feet 4 inches | 25 feet |
| 19 inches | 3 feet 8 inches | 28 feet |
| 20 inches | 4 feet | 30 feet |
| 21 inches | 4 feet 4 inches | 32 feet |

Attaching otter doors to the net is the next step in rigging the trawl gear.

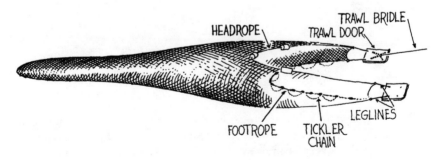

The legline of the footrope (leadline) attaches to the bottom holes behind the doors (see illustration). Leglines of the headrope (corkline) attach to top holes behind the doors. Measure the two lines — the footrope being the longer of the two. Leglines should be connected to the door in such a manner that they can be untied for future adjustment to get maximum performance from the gear. Use a bowline knot for these adjustments. Install floats — if they are not already attached as shown in the "trawl gear" illustration.

Other necessary components of the trawl net rig are trawl bridles and towlines. Each bridle length should be at least three times the length of the headrope. There are basically two types, bridles spliced to a towline:

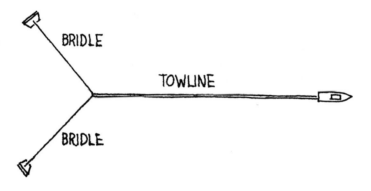

The other is made of two independent bridles:

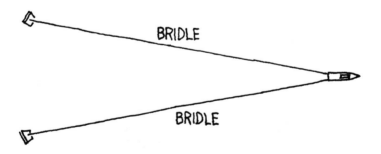

The independent bridles are not spliced into a single headrope and for this reason this system is often favored. If the trawl catches on some obstruction on the bottom, the doors can be retrieved separately. It is important to mention at this point that it is a good idea to attach a highly visible float or plastic jug to the bag of the trawl with a long piece of line or wire. If the net becomes caught on the bottom or lost, it can be retrieved by means of locating the jug or float.

# Setting the Trawl

Now that you've determined what size and type net you need for your boat and motor and now that you've rigged the otter doors; it's time to give it a test run — time to "set the trawl."

One of the first things you must take care to do is be sure that you have carefully coiled the trawl towlines inside the boat so that when they are let out, they will not become tangled with themselves or on other gear, or on any crew members you may have aboard. The bottom of the trawl bag should be tied with a knot that can be easily and quickly untied when a full catch is brought onboard. There is a special knot that was developed just for this use — called the "shrimper's bag knot." Practice tying and untying it before you make your first run.

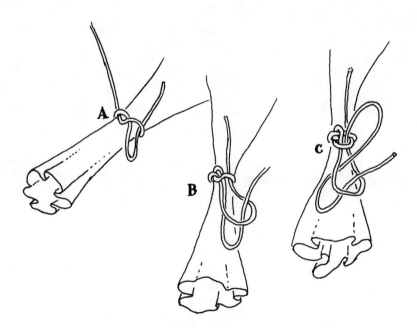

A low, steady speed should be maintained until the trawl and all of its lines are out. Be sure when you set out the otter boards or doors, that they remain in their correct upright position. If not carefully set, they can flip over and twist the leglines. To prevent the doors from floating, they should be completely saturated. Soaking them in water for 24 hours before each use will make them more efficient.

Maintain a light tension on the towline as the doors are set to avoid tangles. Watch the doors to see that they begin to spread the net.

Once the trawl is set, boat speed can be increased. Trawls can be pulled at any speed, but three to four miles per hour is best. The faster trawls catch more shrimp, but the faster the trawl, the more the net tends to lift off the bottom. If it lifts too much, this could cause you to lose some or all of your catch. To correct this, try more weight on the footrope which will help to hold the net closer to the bottom.

After 30 minutes to one hour, you should be ready to haul the net aboard. Working well out of vessel traffic, maneuver the boat to the downwind side of the trawl to keep the lines and other trawl gear from fouling the propeller. Keeping the towline and doors straight, place them in the boat and then haul the net aboard. Now, you can begin sorting your catch. After each use, clean all fish and other debris from the net. Hang the net to allow it to dry thoroughly and store it out of direct sunlight. Net preservatives are frequently sold at net supply houses or hardware stores and the use of a net preservative can help to prolong the life of your net and get more use out of your investment.

# *Trawl Adjustments*

Whether it's your first run or not, gear adjustments must often be made to the doors to control the spread and depth of the trawl and to keep your gear working to the best level of its efficiency.

The chain bridles on the otter board determine its angle assumed in the water, making it one of the primary adjustment points. Here is a common adjustment method used. Extend an imaginary line from the bottom of the door through the first two chain holes:

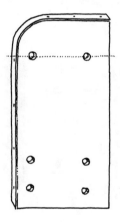

Now, measure from the bottom of the line, a distance 35 to 40 percent of the height of the door.

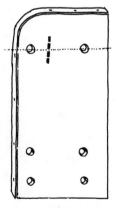

This point is the area where the two back door chains should be attached.:

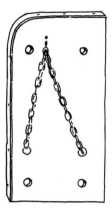

Adjust the top front chain by bringing it down to the center of the bottom from chain hold:

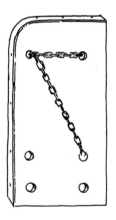

When shrimping, the four door chains are pulled simultaneously and the top back chain should be slightly slack. The top front chain should be one link longer than the bottom front chain and the back top chain should be one link longer than the bottom back chain for the basic adjustment. This allows the doors to tilt to the outside so water pressing against them forces them down. An additional link can be let out on the two top door chains or one taken out on each of the bottom chains if necessary.

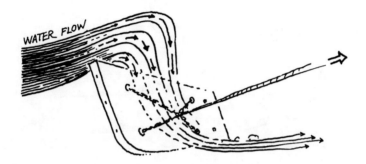

If a greater horizontal angle is needed, other alterations can be made by adjusting the top and bottom back chains. Take these up equally, or for a slightly greater effect, let out the two front chains. Try trawling your net and you should find that after several hours of trawling over a hard or sandy bottom the underside of the doors is shiny from rubbing the bottom.

Another adjustment involves the leglines (the lines which connect the door to the net). These should be adjusted if you find that only the "nose" or the forward portion of the door's bottom is rubbed smooth. Shortening the legline on the top of the door can correct this "nose down" angle. Or you can let out the legline at the bottom of the door.

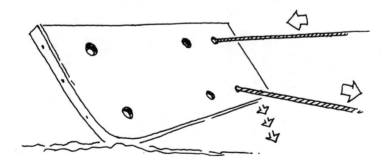

If your problem is the opposite, that is, if you find the extreme back or "heel" of the door becoming rubbed from assuming an improper angle during the trawl, then you'll simply need to reverse the previously detailed legline adjustments. You will either need to loosen the top legline or tighten the bottom legline.

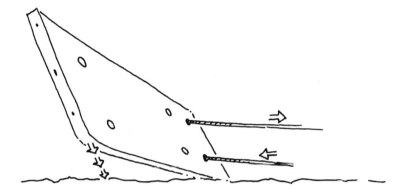

These door adjustments aren't the only modifications you can incorporate into your trawl outfit to increase its efficiency. Floats and weights can be used for specific changes.

For instance, floats — one in the exact center of the headrope or topline along with two more evenly spaced on either side, halfway to the end of the webbing on the headrope — can help increase your catches if you are after the larger white shrimp, by putting the net where the shrimp are, opening it more fully.

Weighting the footrope, to keep the trawl closer to the bottom, can also help increase catches. To accomplish this, you should add two-ounce split lead next to every fourth tie on the footrope (or bottom rope) to weight it.

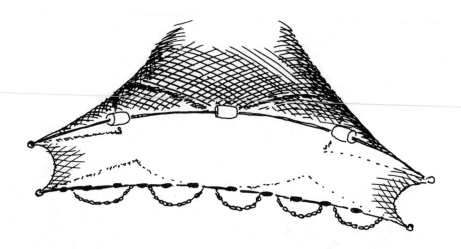

Another trick to boosting your catching involves a bit of trickery. The device — called a "tickler" or jump chain — is simple. It's nothing more than a long ⅜-inch or 3/16-inch chain that is attached to the bottom, at the back, of one of the doors. This tickler drags along the bottom in front of the footrope and scares the shrimp off the bottom, making them more easily caught by the net. Some doors already have a hole for installing a tickler chain, if yours does not, one can easily be drilled.

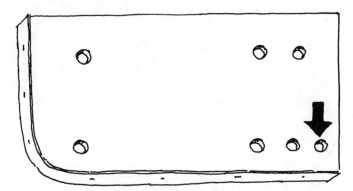

To determine the length of the tickler chain, make it one foot shorter than the length of the footrope which is connected to the doors. The tickler should be shorter than the footrope, but longer than the headrope.

Check you net often for broken mesh. You may snag your net or be faced with wear damage, but these problems can easily be corrected. Minor repairs can be done with a net needle and net twine if there is no webbing missing.

For major net damage, you will need to rebuild the section involved. Working on a flat surface with net twine or heavy fishing line, start at the end of the tear. Using a series of half hitch knots, gather the edges of the tear and without cutting the twine, continue your series of half-hitches as you work across the gap.

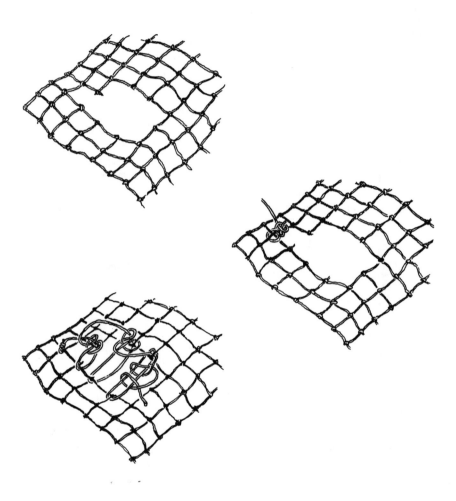

# Handling, Buying and Storing Shrimp

"Living off the fat of the land" sounds like some fictional concept, but this is just what the recreational shrimper does. No shrimp will ever taste better and there can hardly be a greater sense of satisfaction than when you bite into those succulent shrimp — delicacies you've caught by your own hands. That sense of satisfaction will actually increase when you calculate the money you've saved as you package and freeze those pounds of shrimp you've caught.

And we're talking big bucks here, considering the current prices of fresh shrimp. My mother tells me of a time just after World War II when she lived in Jacksonville, Fla. Back then she could get a "big bucket" of shrimp fresh off the shrimp boats at the docks at Mayport for 50 cents. We'll never see those prices again, but a few good runs of shrimp and you can easily repeat those figures — calculating pounds caught against equipment and supplies purchased. Depending upon how many shrimp there are and how persistent a shrimper you are, you can soon recoup much or all of your gear investments and from then on, your catches are essentially free. This, of course, is just looking at recreational shrimping from a purely economical standpoint. But, we're discounting the "recreational" aspect of the sport. For many, shrimping represents more than just a means to an end. It provides enjoyable evenings of sport, companionship and, depending upon the method you chose, either relaxation or exercise.

So, you've given the sport a try and you've caught your first few pounds (or five pounds or 25 pounds or 100 pounds!) of shrimp. You've kept them on ice and now you need to know how to handle this bounty. The first step, is to de-head the shrimp as soon after catching as possible. If done withing an hour or two after catching, the black sand vein which runs along the shrimp's back, will easily pull out as the head is removed.

If you plan to cook your catch you can simply wash the shrimp thoroughly with fresh water and refrigerate until cooking. Fresh, uncooked shrimp can be refrigerated up to three days before use. This should be shortened to two days if you are working with shrimp purchased from a store, since at least a day has been added to its "shelf life" before it reached the store. If you plan to use your shrimp later than that, it is best to freeze them as soon as possible after catching or buying.

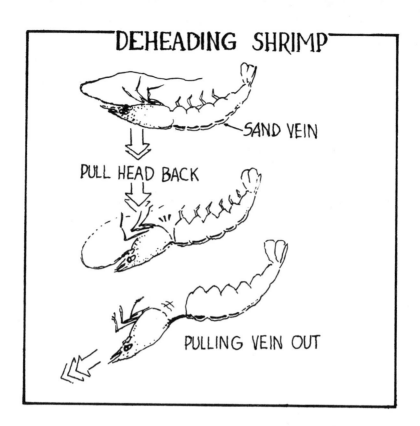

## DEHEADING SHRIMP

SAND VEIN

PULL HEAD BACK

PULLING VEIN OUT

During those short sweet weeks of shrimping season, we keep very late hours at our house. Using cast nets or traps, we'll shrimp until 10 or 11 p.m., depending on how well the shrimp are running and this is often determined by the run of the tide. Then we whisk our catch to the kitchen for processing. Sometimes we'll set aside a pound or two to boil in their shells right away for a snack as we settle down to de-heading and freezer-packing the other 30 pounds or so. Yes, we frequently catch 20 to 30 pounds of shrimp a night during our two- to three-week shrimping season.

The uncooked shrimp freeze better than cooked shrimp, offering a two-fold bonus. We don't have to cook and flash cool a great deal of shrimp to get it ready for the freezer. And also, once defrosted, our shrimp can be prepared in a variety of ways: steamed, simmered, sauteed, barbecued, boiled, stuffed, added to soups, sauces, casseroles, salads, baked or fried. To freeze the shrimp, we (and I say "we" since the catching and processing of this bounty is a family job with everyone pitching in to help) first de-head the shrimp, then wash each with a light spray of water and pack them in plastic freezer containers, leaving the shells on. I've found that even the toughest of the freezer plastic bags is no match for that sharp little spike at the shrimp's tail and those bags routinely are riddled with holes, no matter how carefully we've tried filling them. Throughout the year I save plastic cottage cheese containers (the 24-ounce size holds just about a pound of shrimp and they seal and stack neatly) and other rigid plastic containers for this purpose. They can be discarded after use. Before sealing the plastic container, fill with enough water to cover the shrimp. Don't add anything else, no salt, just fresh water. This is a very important step, because the water seals the shrimp, keeping all air out and it helps the shrimp to retain the freshest possible flavor. I've tried the recommended "book" methods of packing the shrimp dry, but find this usually results in the shrimp obtaining a "freezer" flavor. When frozen in water, shrimp taste very, very close to freshly caught. It also helps prevent freezer burn.

Label each container with contents and date and use within six to eight months. Thaw the shrimp by placing the frozen container in the refrigerator 18 to 24 hours (for a one-pound package) before you plan to use it. If you need to thaw the shrimp quickly, try placing the shrimp-filled block of ice in a colander. Run cold, never warm or hot, water over it to melt the ice, carefully separating the shrimp as the ice melts. Don't thaw shrimp at room temperature because, besides the possibility of bacteria growth the shrimp can lose flavor, moisture and freshness. These steps also apply to commercially frozen and packaged shrimp, many brands of which will come already cooked and shelled. Never re-freeze shrimp once they've been defrosted.

If you plan to boil the shrimp, it is best NOT to shell it first. The shrimp may be de-headed, but not shelled for best results. Cooking the shrimp in its shell gives the cooked shrimp a richer pink color and a more natural curve. But, most important, it seems to have a better flavor and texture and shrimp cooked in its shell won't shrink as much as shelled shrimp does. We'll discuss cooking shrimp in more detail in the next chapter.

You've no doubt noticed there is a lot of waste associated with getting your shrimp from the water to your table. If you are especially frugal, I'd suggest you use the heads and shells to produce a delicate shrimp court boullion (see recipe section). At my house, the hundreds and hundreds of shrimp heads and later shells which we remove, frequently go into the compost pile to eventually enrich our vegetable and flower gardens.

If you'd like to be able to calculate just how much shrimp you'll have after the "green" (that means raw shrimp with heads and shells) shrimp are cleaned and cooked, here's a chart which should prove helpful when planning a meal or even when purchasing fresh shrimp.

| Pounds of "Green" Shrimp | Shelled White Shrimp | Shelled Brown Shrimp | Shelled Pink Shrimp |
|---|---|---|---|
| 1 lb. (heads on) | .65 lb. | .62 lb. | .63 lb. |
| 2 lbs. (heads on) | 1.95 lbs. | 1.86 lbs. | 1.89 lbs. |
| 3 lbs. (heads on) | 3.25 lbs. | 3.10 lbs. | 3.15 lbs. |

These figures will vary slightly, depending upon sizes of shrimp. There are four commercial classifications:

| | |
|---|---|
| Jumbo | 10 to 15 per pound |
| Large | 15 to 30 per pound |
| Medium | 30 to 42 per pound |
| Small | 42 or more per pound |

Generally one to two pounds of shrimp, in the shell and de-headed, will serve four if cooked in a main dish with additional seafood and /or vegetables. But for fried or boiled shrimp you will need at least a dozen or more, depending on the size of the shrimp and the appetites per person.

Like most seafoods, shrimp pack a real nutritional punch, being an excellent source of protein, containing about 18.1 percent protein, .8 percent fat and 1.5 percent carbohydrates. Shrimp also have a goodly share of B vitamins and minerals, namely iodine, phosphorus, calcium and copper. Calorie count varies, according to preparation. But basically, 3½ ounces of uncooked shrimp, about an average serving size, has 90 calories, while 3½ ounces of frozen breaded shrimp have 140 calories. Fresh fried and battered shrimp have 225 calories per 3½-ounce serving.

Although nearly 90 percent of the annual shrimp harvest is frozen for use in restaurants and to be sold in supermarkets, fresh shrimp is readily available in fish markets and at supermarket seafood counters in most areas, year round. All shrimp are highly perishable and when purchasing fresh shrimp you should look for firm-fleshed shrimp with a mild or no odor. Avoid any with a strong or iodine odor. The flesh should be translucent and free of spots and shouldn't be slippery or slimy looking. If you are purchasing frozen shrimp, make sure they are solidly frozen, with little or no odor, no brown spots and no signs of freezer burn, indicated by a very white, dry appearance around the edges.

Another way to buy shrimp is in the can. The standard 4½-ounce can will yield approximately one measuring cup of shrimp which are already cooked, shelled and de-veined. They are usually quite small. Just rinse the slightly salty brine from the canned shrimp and use as desired in recipes calling for cooked shrimp. These tiny shrimp are often just the right size to add to canned soups, like cream of tomato, cream of asparagus and so on. Just be sure to add them just before serving to avoid overcooking them. When rinsing canned shrimp, do it quickly and in cool water. Never soak canned shrimp in lukewarm water. As a bonus, the mildly salted, shrimp-flavored liquid (about one-third of a cup) in which the shrimp are packed, can be added to sauces or used to replace a portion of the liquids called for in recipes. Canned shrimp has a shelf life of one year.

If you are faced with a bonanza of freshly-caught shrimp and don't have the facilities for freezing it, you might want to consider canning it yourself. While freezing is by far the best method for preserving shrimp — easier, safer and results in a far superior product — canning shrimp in a brine solution is a viable alternative. Because fish and shellfish are high on the danger list as prime candidates for botulism contamination, shellfish canners must adhere strictly to recommended canning techniques. Only new, modern, straight-sided, one-half and one-pint jars and two-piece screwband lids, all in perfect condition, can be used. A pressure canner must be used due to extra long and specific processing requirements for this type of shrimp processing. A canning thermometer is necessary also.

The shrimp must first be shelled and de-veined if the sand vein is present.

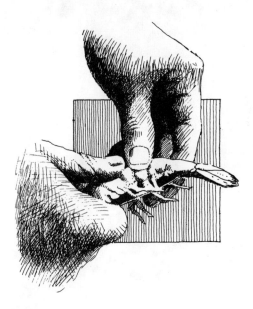

*Hold the shrimp with your left hand with the swimmerettes (or underside) facing upwards. With your right hand, place the blade of the knife along the inside of the swimmerettes nearest you.*

*Then with your left hand, turn the shrimp away from you. The blade should cut through the shell, which should start to peel.*

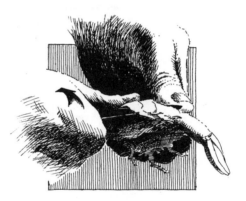

*Keep twisting.*

*There. The shell is off. Drop the shell and then with your right hand, point the tail of the shrimp to your right hand and using your thumb and one of your fingers pinch out the meat from the tail. Slit the shrimp along its back to expose the sand vein — if not already removed — and wash it away with a fine spray of water.*

When all the shrimp are shelled and cleaned, you will need to prepare the brine. Dissolve two cups pure pickling salt to each gallon of water. Place the shrimp in a large enameled kettle and add enough brine to cover and soak the shrimp in this solution for 25 to 30 minutes, stirring from time to time. Then drain shrimp.

Next, you must acid-blanch the shrimp to keep the flesh from darkening. Combine one cup pure pickling salt and one cup lemon juice for each gallon of water. If you are processing several pounds of shrimp, you'll need to mix several gallons of this because it cannot be re-used for subsequent batches. Half fill a deep-frying basket with shrimp. Then, in a pot large enough to accomodate the basket, boil enough acid blanch to cover the basket when it is immersed. Continue to boil the shrimp for six to eight minutes, depending on the size of the shrimp. Drain, then cool and air-dry shrimp on wire racks. The shrimp need to be dry to the touch and cool when packed in one-half pint jars. Fit shrimp carefully into the jars to get a solid pack, without crushing shrimp. Add boiling water to cover shrimp. There should be one-half inch of headroom in jars. Half-close jars, that is, screw the band down over the flat lid just until the band cannot be pulled up off the threads.

In a pressure canner, exhaust the jars at zero pounds until the inside of the pack reaches at least 170 degrees F or 77 degrees C on a thermometer. This will take about 10 minutes. Next, screw bands tight and then pressure process the one-half pint jars at 10 pounds until they reach 240 degrees F or 116 degrees C. This should take about 35 minutes. Remove jars from canner and allow them to air cool.

Although the very efficient freeze-drying method has been used successfully for years to produce a fishing bait, this process has not been used as a means for preserving shrimp for use as a food. Besides, freeze-drying takes expensive and sophisticated equipment, making it unsuitable as a home-based process. However, dried shrimp, which has been brine-treated and air-dried is frequently found in Oriental markets. This method of preserving shrimp is popular in some sections of the world where there is little or no refrigeration. In this process the shrimp lose about 90 percent of their weight. While inferior in taste and texture to fresh or fresh frozen shrimp, in many countries and for specific purposes (like camping trip food, etc.) the drying of shrimp can be viewed as a good method for supplying protein. It is cheaper to process shrimp by drying than by canning and as an added bonus, large commercial shrimp drying operations (namely in Mexico) have salvaged the wastes — about 40 percent of the total weight of unprocessed shrimp — for a by-product side industry. Those wastes from the shrimp, scraps and shells, are made into poultry feed and a fishing bait. In this Mexican industry the "green" shrimp are boiled in a brine solution and dried in the open air. This process takes about three to four days and is very labor-intensive as the shrimp must be turned frequently and covered at night. Then they are deheaded, peeled, sprinkled with a sugar mixture and packed in barrels for transport.

when hiking or camping.

As with all these methods described for preserving shrimp from freezing to canning to drying, use only fresh shrimp in excellent condition.

Prepare a brine of one-half cup salt and one quart of water. Cover about two pounds of medium to small cleaned, shelled and deveined shrimp with this mixture and soak for 30 minutes.

While the shrimp are soaking, prepare a dry cure mixture of one tablespoon salt, one teaspoon ground allspice, one tablespoon mixed pickling spices, two crushed dry bay leaves, two medium onions sliced and two tablespoons white vinegar, mixing well. Rinse the brine from the shrimp and coat with the dry cure mixture. Place in an airtight glass or plastic container and refrigerate four to eight hours.

Arrange the shrimp on drying trays and dry for 12 to 14 hours at 145 degrees until dry. The shrimp should feel dry and tough and have no moist spots. The shrimp should not crumble. Pack dried shrimp loosely in airtight containers and refrigerate for up to three months or freeze for up to six months.

Another option is to smoke the shrimp. Large to jumbo shrimp are suggested for this method in which you can choose a brine or a dry cure.

To brine cure you begin by combining two cups salt and one gallon water. Soak four to six pounds of shelled and deveined shrimp in this for 30 minutes. While this is soaking, prepare a second brine of one pound of salt, one cup sugar, one cup lemon juice, one teaspoon garlic powder, one-third cup mixed pickling spices, one teaspoon pepper, two cups cider vinegar and one and one-half quarts of water. Stir to dissolve and soak the shrimp in this second brine for two to four hours in the refrigerator, weighting the top to keep the shrimp submerged.

To dry cure you need to thickly coat three to four pounds of large to jumbo shrimp which have been shelled and deveined with this mixture: one pound of salt, two cups brown sugar, one teaspoon ground allspice, one teaspoon ground cloves, two teaspoons crushed dry bay leaves and one tablespoon onion powder. Place shrimp in a shallow covered container and refrigerate for four to eight hours.

After curing with either of the above two methods, rinse the shrimp and pat dry. Use a temperature-controlled smokehouse or smoking oven. Lightly smoke the shrimp for six hours at 80 to 90 degrees with the draft and flue open. Densely smoke the shrimp for two more hours, gradually raising the temperature to 130 degrees F to 150 degrees F. Hold at this temperature one and a half to two hours or until the shrimp have a shiny brown surface. Place a meat thermometer in the shrimp and increase the oven temperature to 225 degrees F until the meat thermometer reaches 180 degrees F. Maintain this temperature for 30 minutes to inhibit the growth of bacteria which can cause food poisoning. Cool the shrimp for one to two hours and while they are still warm, brush with vegetable oil. Wrap cooled shrimp in wax paper and then in freezer paper and freeze for storage up to six months. Depending on size of shrimp, you may need to adjust smoking times to prevent overdrying. Shrimp should be leathery in texture, not crumble when handled.

# Addendum — Technical Characterization of Shrimp

Shrimp, along with lobsters and crabs, belong to the phylum *Arthropoda;* the super-class *Crustacea,* the class *Malacostraca* and the order *Decapoda.* Breaking that down, we find that shrimp (lobsters and crabs) aren't the only members of the phylum *Arthropoda.* They are joined by insects, spiders and horseshoe crabs. The Latin term *Arthropoda* describes members of a group of animals which have jointed appendages. Characteristically, Arthropods are bilaterally symmetrical; that is, the right and left halves of the body are the same — mirror images. All animals in the phylum have a hard exterior covering for their body, an exoskeleton or shell. The shell of the shrimp for example, is bilaterally symmetrical and hard, but not as hard as a crab's or lobster's shell. The shrimp's body is segmented with 38 segments. The shrimp's exoskeleton is composed of chitin which is a chemical compound, protein and compounds of calcium. It is the pliable non-calcified chitin and protein membranes which make up part of the joints of these animals; the exoskeletons have flexible appendage joints.

The exoskeletons of shrimp are a mixed blessing. While they provide the animal with some degree of protection, they also must be shed as the animals grow since their shells cannot expand as the body enlarges. Called ecdysis, this shedding or casting off the old shell must be accomplished many times during the life cycle as the shrimp grows from a microscopic plankton speck called a larva.

In the biological list, the shrimp is an Arthropod which is part of the super-class called Crustacea. This Latin term emphasizes the animal's hard shell or "crust." Along with shrimp, lobster and crabs and certain insects are also in this class. Physical characteristics, common to them, include those already discussed as belonging to Arthropods but closing the gap is that Crustacea all have a pair of mandibles — that is, cutting or crushing jaws. Shrimp, like their cousin lobsters and crabs, have two pairs of antennae.

Further defining its place on the family tree, the shrimp belongs to the class *Malacostra* which are in the order *Decapoda* (lobster and crab). The shrimp has compound eyes on stalks, 38 body segments (19 in the body, five in the head, eight in the thorax and six in the abdomen).

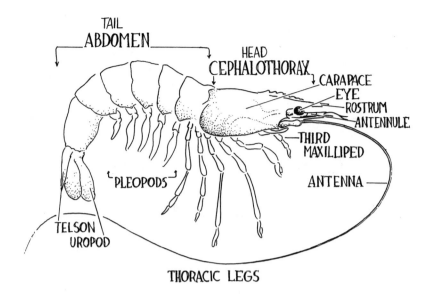

TAIL
ABDOMEN
HEAD
CEPHALOTHORAX
CARAPACE
EYE
ROSTRUM
ANTENNULE
THIRD
MAXILLIPED
PLEOPODS
ANTENNA
TELSON
UROPOD
THORACIC LEGS

Like other Decapods, the shrimp has 10 feet. On its head, the shrimp has two feelers or antennules; next are mandibles, another pair of appendages located just outside the mouth. The shrimp's accessory jaws or maxillae constitute the fourth and fifth pair of appendages and the maxillipeds are sixth through eighth pairs of appendages which assist in the ingestion of food. Five pairs of walking legs (some may have claws in certain species of shrimp) are followed by five more pairs of appendages (making 10 feet), which are swimmerets. The final pair of appendages is called the uropods which form the tailfan along with the telson.

Species of shrimp vary in coloration, some extremely colorful, others quite drab, and they vary in size from tiny shrimp to huge fist-sized wonders. But these basic characteristics can be used to describe our quarry no matter where we seek it.

With a life expectancy of one year, I find the story of the shrimp life cycle both sad and joyous — sad, because it is so brief and yet joyous because the short-lived shrimp reproduces with such wild abandon, with females of some species laying up to 1,000,000 eggs. Only a small percentage will in turn live to reproduce. This paradox is both discouraging and yet hopeful at the same time. As one researcher put it to me, "We are just lucky that they reproduce so well." Indeed we are!

# Cooking Shrimp
# — Recipes

*"If you would relish food, labor for it before you take it..." Benjamin Franklin.*

Up to this point you've gone to a certain amount of labor to obtain your fresh shrimp and you want to use it to its best advantage. One of the worst culinary sins is to overcook shrimp. Perhaps this is done so frequently because it is so easy to do. During cooking, the watery juices of the shrimp become milky and the flesh becomes opaque and white with pink accents. The color change is unmistakable and is usually accomplished in three to five minutes. You may choose a variety of cooking methods, but with shrimp you must always remember to be careful not to overcook.

While chefs and cooks everywhere agree on the need to cook shrimp with tender loving care, they seem divided on whether to shell or not to shell the shrimp before cooking. They also can't seem to agree on whether or not to salt the water in which shrimp are boiled. I tend to concur with the latter of both arguments. To repeat a statement I've already made earlier in this book, shrimp cooked in the shell not only look better, but taste better and have a better texture also. This is especially true when steaming or boiling shrimp. I also prefer to boil my shrimp sans any salt in the water. I believe the addition of salt to the boiling water only serves to toughen the shrimp. Of course, there will be times, when preparing deep-fried battered or breaded shrimp for example, when pre-shelling is a must, but always go easy on the salt before and during cooking of shrimp.

Let's start with the basics of cooking shrimp. Many of the recipes which follow will call for pre-cooked shrimp to be added to cold sauces or to be used in sandwiches or in salads. That means boiled shrimp. Here again, there are two schools of method on this matter. I have always had excellent luck with briskly boiling fresh shrimp in the shell for three to five minutes. The only problem I've encountered is a pot readily inclined to boil over with a frothy mixture of water and shrimp "scum." But as far as the quality of the cooked shrimp prepared in this manner goes, I've found no difference from shrimp prepared by simmering -- the choice of many cooks. I guess it's just a force of habit that I choose to boil rather than simmer. But here are your options:

# Boiled Shrimp

2 pounds raw shrimp, de-headed but unpeeled
    (thawed if frozen)
8 cups boiling water in large pot

Have pot no more than one-half full of boiling water. While water is briskly boiling, add shrimp all at once. Continue to boil over medium-heat for three to five minutes, or until shrimp are done. Test for doneness by cutting a shrimp in half. Flesh should be opaque in center when done. Quickly drain all water from pot and if you plan to serve it hot, serve immediately. If you plan to use the shrimp in a recipe calling for cooked shrimp, rinse the shrimp with cold water to cool and then peel shrimp, removing sand vein if necessary. Use as called for.

# Simmered Shrimp

2 pounds raw, de-headed, unpeeled shrimp
    (thawed if frozen)
8 cups water

In a large pot, bring water to a boil. Add shrimp all at once and reduce heat. Cover and simmer for three to five minutes, or until shrimp are done. Test for doneness by cutting a shrimp in half. Flesh should be opaque in center when done. Quickly drain all water from pot and if you plan to serve shrimp hot, serve immediately. If you plan to use the shrimp in a recipe calling for cooked shrimp, rinse the shrimp with cold water to cool and then peel shrimp, removing sand vein if necessary. Use as called for.

I spoke earlier in this book of a use for those shells and heads to prepare a delicate shrimp broth. You need to save enough shrimp shells to make ¾ of a pound. This is quite a lot of the shells, since they weigh little. Store them in the freezer, if need be, until you have accumulated enough. The recipe is simple to prepare and the stock can be used as a base for a number of soups, chowders or casseroles. The broth can be frozen up to three months.

# Shrimp Shell Stock

3 cups, or ¾ pound shrimp shells, uncooked
1 small onion, sliced
1 carrot, sliced
3 whole peppercorns
1 bay leaf
1 whole allspice
2 sprigs fresh parsley or 2 teaspoons dried parsley
¾ teaspoon salt
5 cups boiling water

Combine all ingredients in a large pan and bring to a boil. Cover and simmer 30 minutes. Strain before using in soups or sauces.

Sure, those boiled shrimp in the shells create quite a sensation with your family or guests when you set heaping platters before them, but as good as they are, there are times when something a bit more fancy — something different — is called for. Shrimp can take you from dainty (or robust) appetizers to sandwiches to soups and chowders to salads to main dishes, and all in very good taste. Shrimp is the seafood for even those who say they don't like seafood. Everyone loves shrimp, well, maybe not everyone, but just about everyone. We've got our basics behind us and now it's time to move on to those delicious dishes that make the most of shrimp.

# *Appetizers*

*The nationally-known Columbia Restaurant of Tampa, Fla., is famous for its bacon-wrapped fried shrimp. While this may not be the exact recipe, it is a close copy of this delicacy that is often used as a garnish for the Columbia's seafood dishes. These tasty fried shrimp are also great appetizers.*

## Bacon-wrapped Shrimp

16 large or jumbo shrimp, peeled and deveined
8 thin strips of bacon, split lengthwise
2 eggs, lightly beaten
½ cup milk
Flour, seasoned with salt, pepper and dash garlic salt

Wrap each shrimp with strip of bacon and secure with a toothpick. Beat together eggs and milk and dip shrimp. Then roll shrimp in seasoned flour.

Heat shortening to 300 degrees and deep fry shrimp until golden, about six minutes. Drain on paper toweling.

*Cool and refreshing, these pickled shrimp are one of my family's favorites. So pretty, this dish makes a special company presentation on the appetizer table or can even go it alone for a cooling summer entree. This recipe was developed shortly after an especially bountiful shrimping season. We literally had shrimp coming out of our ears and had tired of all our usual favorite recipes. Yes, you CAN have too much shrimp, but this flavorful rendition sparked up even our jaded appetites.*

## Pickled Shrimp

2 pounds shrimp, cooked, then shelled and deveined, leave tails on
1 onion, thinly sliced and separated into rings
¼ cup pitted black olives
¼ cup pimiento-stuffed green olives
¼ cup cider vinegar
½ cup vegetable oil
1 lemon, sliced
¼ cup lemon juice
¼ chopped parsley
1 tablespoon Dijon-style mustard
1 bay leaf
¼ teaspoon garlic powder
1 tablespoon fresh basil or one teaspoon crumbled dried basil
¼ teaspoon freshly ground black pepper

Lightly toss shrimp, onion, olives and sliced lemon in glass salad bowl.

In a jar, combine remaining ingredients and shake well in mix. Pour over shrimp mixture. Cover bowl with plastic wrap and refrigerate overnight to marinate, tossing occasionally. Serve well chilled. Serves six to eight.


## Marinated Shrimp I

3 pounds cooked, shelled and deveined shrimp
1 ¼ cups vegetable oil
⅓ cup cider vinegar
½ cup catsup
2 teaspoons sugar
3 teaspoons Worcestershire sauce
2 cloves garlic
2 teaspoons dry mustard
¼ teaspoon freshly ground pepper
⅛ teaspoon bottled hot pepper sauce, more if desired
1 large onion, sliced thinly and separated into rings
4 bay leaves

Place shrimp in large glass bowl. Combine the next nine ingredients in food processor or blender and process until smooth. Pour over shrimp in bowl, add onions and bay leaves and toss lightly. Cover and refrigerate and marinate two days. Serve cold, garnished with parsley sprigs if desired. Serves 12.

*Marinating shrimp is indeed popular, as the following variations can attest. Here's another recipe for this favorite, which is served chilled as is the previous recipe. Following it are two variations, but they are to be served hot. Take your pick, or try them all.*

# Marinated Shrimp II

2 pounds shrimp, cooked, shelled and deveined
1 teaspoon minced seeded fresh or pickled hot pepper or
1/8 teaspoon crushed red pepper, or to taste
1 cup fresh lime juice
1 teaspoon salt
2 bay leaves
1/4 teaspoon cumin seeds
1 medium red onion, sliced and separated into rings
1/4 cup pitted black olives, cut in halves

In a large glass or ceramic bowl, combine all ingredients, except for shrimp. Add shrimp, tossing lightly. Cover and refrigerate over night to marinate. Serves 12.

# Hot Marinated Shrimp I

3 pounds large shrimp, uncooked and in the shell
3 quarts water
1 large onion, quartered
1/2 lemon, sliced thinly
4 stalks celery
1/2 cup dry white wine
1/2 teaspoon thyme leaves, crumbled
1 teaspoon basil leaves, crumbled
2 bay leaves
4 cloves garlic, split
Few drops bottled liquid hot pepper sauce, to taste

Combine all ingredients, except for shrimp, in a large pot and bring to boil. Add shrimp. Return to boiling and then reduce heat and simmer five minutes or until shrimp turn pink and are done through. Drain and serve hot as is or with a garlic-butter sauce to dip shrimp. Serves 12.

# Hot Marinated Shrimp II

3 pounds raw shrimp in shells
10 whole peppercorns
4 cloves garlic
1 teaspoon whole cloves
3 lemons, sliced thinly
1/4 teaspoon cayenne pepper

1 large green pepper, chopped, but not seeded
4 bay leaves
1 tablespoon salt
1 teaspoon celery seed
1 cup cider or tarragon vinegar
1½ gallons water

Combine all ingredients, except for shrimp, in a large pot and bring to a boil. Boil for 15 minutes and then add shrimp and cover. Reduce heat and simmer about eight minutes, or until shrimp are done.

Drain and serve immediately with your favorite cocktail sauce or garlic butter.

## Shrimp Saute Parmesan

1 pound raw, peeled and deveined small to medium shrimp
1 teaspoon chopped chives
1 clove garlic, minced
¼ cup butter or margarine
2 tablespoons dry sherry
3 tablespoons grated Parmesan cheese

Melt butter in a 10-inch skillet and saute chives and garlic until just soft. Add shrimp and saute' over medium high heat for two to three minutes, or until the largest shrimp is opaque in the center. Add sherry, stirring and top with Parmesan cheese. Serve warm with toothpicks. Serves eight to ten.

## Lime Shrimp

1 pounds, cooked, shelled and deveined shrimp
1 cup fresh lime juice, or enough to cover shrimp
2 tablespoons each minced green pepper and onion
1 tomato, chopped
1 cucumber, peeled, seeded and chipped
½ cup tomato juice
Pepper and hot pepper sauce to taste

Combine shrimp and lime juice and marinate one hour in refrigerator. Drain shrimp, reserving lime juice. Combine juice with other ingredients and serve in small bowls as a dipping sauce for shrimp. Serves four to six.

# Hot Dilled Shrimp

2 cups shelled raw shrimp
¼ cup butter or margarine
1 clove garlic, minced
1 teaspoon dried dillweed
Shrimp sauce (recipe follows)

In a skillet or chafing dish, melt butter and saute' garlic. Add dillweed and shrimp. Cook, stirring frequently, about five to eight minutes, or until shrimp are done. Serve hot with following sauce:

### Shrimp Sauce, combine:

1 cup bottled chilled sauce
¼ cup sauterne
2 tablespoons snipped fresh parsley

*The following is one of the recipes Robert H. Robinson devised for using the tiny grass shrimp, available in so many areas. Broken, small or chopped shrimp can be substituted in this tasty appetizer.*

# Shrimplet Puffs

1 cup of shrimplets (heads on) which have been boiled for one minute or one cup of shrimp pieces
½ cup all-purpose flour
1 egg
1 tablespoon soy sauce
½ cup milk

Make a batter of the flour, egg, soy sauce and milk and stir in shrimp. Using a tablespoon, drop spoonfuls of batter into hot oil and cook until puffs are brown. Drain. You may want to dip puffs in a hot red sauce or tartar sauce, but Robinson enjoys them unadorned. Serves two to four.

*The traditional appetizer and standby, shrimp cocktail, is a pretty straightforward affair — chilled, peeled, boiled shrimp and served with a tomato-based cocktail sauce, usually laced with horseradish. The shrimp can be presented simply, on a plate or in a bowl, or lavishly in specially designed shrimp cocktail dishes which have a two-part construction to hold crushed ice in the bottom portion so that the shrimp does not sit on the ice, eliminating the possibility of it getting wet or soggy. Or, the shrimp can be presented in an elaborate ice sculpture or a ring of ice in which seashells have been frozen. The effect is stunning and simple to achieve. Here's a variation with a piquante sauce that could just replace that old bottled variety at your house.*

## Shrimp Cocktail Supreme

**2 pounds cooked, cleaned and shelled shrimp**
**½ cup olive oil**
**1 tablespoon horseradish**
**3 tablespoons paprika**
**1 tablespoon prepared mustard**
**1 teaspoon celery seed**
**¼ teaspoon pepper**
**¼ teaspoon onion or garlic powder**
**¼ cup vinegar, preferably tarragon**

Arrange chilled shrimp in serving dishes. Combine remaining ingredients and serve, well-chilled, in small bowls with shrimp. Serves six.

## Shrimp Fritters

**1 cup chopped, cooked shrimp, fresh, frozen or canned**
**4 eggs, separated**
**½ teaspoon celery salt**
**1 tablespoon chopped parsley**
**2 tablespoons flour**
**Hot oil for frying**

Beat egg yolks with celery salt, parsley and flour. Beat egg whites until stiff and fold into egg yolk mixture. Add shrimp.

Drop approximately ¼ cup batter into hot oil and deep fry until golden. Drain and serve immediately with this hot Tomato Sauce:

**2 tablespoons olive oil**
**1 10-ounce can tomatoes and green chilies**
**1 onion, chopped**

1 clove garlic, minced
¼ teaspoon freshly ground pepper

Saute onion and garlic in olive oil in a skillet. Add tomatoes and chilies and pepper and bring to a boil. Reduce heat and simmer, covered, 20 minutes. Serve warm with fritters.


*A variation of the shrimp fritter is the shrimp ball, also deep fried in a batter. The by-word here is small, usually measuring out the seafood-chocked batter by spoonfuls. Serve with a cocktail sauce.*


## Shrimp Balls

1½ pounds minced raw shrimp
1 medium onion, grated
1 medium potato, unpeeled and grated
1 egg
Salt and pepper to taste
Hot oil for deep frying

Combine all ingredients, except oil, to form a thick batter. Drop by spoonfuls into the hot oil and fry until golden brown. Drain and serve hot with a cocktail sauce. Serves six to eight.


## Shrimp-Crab Cheese Tart

¼ cup mayonnaise
2 tablespoons lemon juice
2 eight-ounce packages cream cheese, softened
1 teaspoon Worcestershire sauce
Dash garlic powder
2 tablespoons chopped chives
⅔ cup chopped celery
2 tablespoons sweet pickle relish
¾ cup bottled chili sauce
1 six-ounce can crab meat, drained and cartilage removed
1 four and a half-ounce can shrimp, drained
¼ cup chopped fresh parsley
Crackers

Beat together the mayonnaise, lemon juice, cream cheese, Worcestershire sauce and garlic powder until smooth. Spread and flatten into a nine-inch round on a platter. Combine the relish and chili sauce and spread on top of cheese mixture. Arrange crab and shrimp on top and sprinkle with chopped parsley. Serve well chilled with assorted crackers. Serves 18 to 20.

*Shrimp pastes and butters differ from shrimp dips in that they usually call for mincing or even pureeing the shrimp to create a smooth mixture. In the Deep South shrimp pastes and butters were traditionally served at breakfast, but these delicate mixtures take to the appetizer selections equally as well. Here's a trio for you to select from, the first being another of R. Robinson's uses for tiny grass shrimp.*

## Shrimplet Butter

½ cup shrimplets, heads on
8 tablespoons butter

Melt butter and stir in shrimp. Cook until shrimp turn pink. Cool and turn into blended or bowl of food processor. Process until the mixture is creamy. Spread on bread and toast in the oven or spread on toast. You can chill and freeze the remainder to use on toast or to add to any creamy soup. This is rich stuff and a little bit goes a long way.

## Shrimp Paste

2 pounds fresh shrimp in shells
Boiling water
1 clove garlic
1 bay leaf
½ cup wine vinegar
½ pound softened butter
½ teaspoon mace
1 teaspoon onion juice
Chopped fresh parsley

Cook shrimp in the boiling water to which you have added the garlic, bay leaf and vinegar. Drain and cool shrimp. Shell shrimp and chop coarsley and cream with softened butter, mace and onion juice. Turn into a serving bowl, adding salt to taste. Garnish with the chopped parsley and a few of the whole shrimp. Serve with crackers or spread on Melba toast.

# Old South Shrimp Paste

2 cans (4 ½ ounces) shrimp or ½ pound cooked,
  peeled shrimp, chilled
½ cup butter
2 tablespoons dry sherry
1 tablespoon grated onion
¼ teaspoon mace
1 tablespoon lemon juice
¼ teaspoon dry mustard
¼ teaspoon cayenne pepper

Grind chilled shrimp in finest blade of food grinder or in food processor. Cream butter and beat in sherry, onion, mace, lemon juice, dry mustard and pepper. Add shrimp, beating until smooth. Serve with assorted crackers or Melba toast.

*Probably one of the first ways that shrimp appeared on the appetizer scene was in the form of a dip. Shrimp dips are a delicious and easy way to serve this delicate shellfish to your guests. Here are a few variations for you to sample. Try them with crackers, Melba toast or with chips.*

# House Specialty Shrimp Dip

1 ½ pounds cooked, peeled shrimp
1 16-ounce container whipped cream cheese
1 tablespoon Worcestershire sauce
1 ½ teaspoons bottled hot pepper sauce
1 cup mayonnaise
2 tablespoons chopped chives

Coarsley chop shrimp and combine with remaining ingredients. Chill several hours or overnight to blend flavors. Makes three cups.

# Pink Shrimp Dip

½ pound shrimp, cooked and cleaned and chopped
2 cups sour cream
¼ cup bottled chili sauce
1 package dry onion soup mix, 1 ¾ ounces
1 tablespoon chopped parsley

Combine all ingredients, except for the parsley which is used as a garnish. Mix thoroughly and chill. Serve with assorted crackers. Makes 3 ¼ cups dip.

# Artichoke-Shrimp Dip

1 pound cooked, cleaned and chopped shrimp
1 14-ounce can artichoke hearts, rinsed, drained and chopped
1 medium onion, chopped
1 cup sour cream
1 cup mayonnaise
¼ cup bottled chili sauce
1 tablespoon Worcestershire sauce
1 drop hot bottled pepper sauce

Combine all ingredients and chill overnight. Serve cold with assorted crackers or Melba toast. Makes about four cups dip.

# Garden Shrimp Dip (for a crowd)

2 cups chopped green onions, tops included
½ cup each green pepper and celery, chopped
1 small jar pimientos, drained and chopped coarsley
2 tablespoons butter or margarine
2 ½ pounds raw shrimp, shelled and cleaned
2 cans cream of mushroom soup
Garlic powder and cayenne pepper to taste

Saute onions, green pepper, celery, and pimientos in the butter. Add shrimp which have been cut in halves or thirds and cook about one minute. Add soup and simmer until shrimp are cooked through, about eight to 10 minutes. Season to taste with garlic powder and pepper and serve warm with crackers or Melba toast. Makes about four to five cups dip.

# Hot Shrimp-Cheese Dip

1 pound raw shrimp, shelled and chopped
½ cup butter or margarine, melted
½ cup chopped green onion with tops
¼ cup chopped green pepper
1 pound mild cheddar cheese, diced
1 tablespoon dry sherry
½ cup bottled chili sauce
1 tablespoon Worcestershire sauce
Pepper to taste
2 drops liquid hot pepper sauce, or to taste

Combine the shrimp with the butter, onion and green pepper in a medium saucepan. Saute to cook shrimp and vegetables, about five minutes. In another pan, combine the cheese, sherry, chili sauce, Worcestershire sauce, pepper and hot pepper sauce and heat slowly to melt cheese. This can be done in a microwave oven cooking on "medium" for four minutes. Combine shrimp and cheese mixtures and heat through. Serve hot with chips, crackers or chunks of raw vegetables for dipping. Makes three cups.

# *Salads*

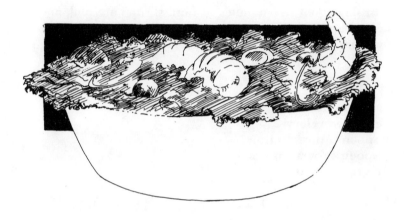

# Shrimp Salad in Lettuce Cups

Bouquet garni:
   2 tablespoons shrimp spice or mixed pickling spices
   1 tablespoon parsley or one sprig fresh
   1 bay leaf
   1 tablespoon salt
   3 tablespoons cider vinegar
   1 stalk celery with leaves

Bring six cups water to boil and add bouquet garni, add:

**1½ pounds fresh or frozen, defrosted, shrimp, unpeeled**

Boil briskly about five minutes or until shrimp are pink and done. Drain. Peel and devein shrimp. Sprinkle with one-quarter cup tarragon vinegar. Cool for about one half hour. Combine following ingredients and toss with shrimp:

3 hard boiled eggs, coarsely chopped
¼ cup mayonnaise
1 cup chopped celery
1 tablespoon minced onion
1 tablespoon capers, drained
Freshly ground pepper.

Chill well and serve in lettuce cups. Serves six to eight.


# Congealed Shrimp Salad

½ cup cold water
2 one-tablespoon envelopes unflavored gelatin
1 cup mayonnaise
¼ cup sliced green olives
1 pound cooked, cleaned shrimp
2 teaspoons horseradish
2 teaspoons minced onion
¼ cup lemon juice
¼ teaspoon paprika
1 cup commercial sour cream

Combine water and gelatin to soften. Stir in mayonnaise and then other ingredients. Turn into gelatin mold and chill until congealed. Serves six.

*There are many versions of this succulent shrimp salad, this one is a bit different and has a Mediterranean accent. If you can't obtain the Greek olives, then substitute black olives.*

## Shrimp Louis

4 cups cooked and cleaned shrimp
Leaf lettuce
1 quart shredded iceburg lettuce
2 ripe tomatoes, quartered
1 dozen Greek ripe olives or black olives
1 green pepper, sliced into rings
2 cups chick peas
Shrimp Louis Dressing

Arrange three or four lettuce leaves on each of four plates. Divide iceberg lettuce between the four plates. Arrange shrimp over shredded lettuce. Garnish with remaining ingredients. Top with dressing:

### Shrimp Louis Dressing

1 ½ cups chili sauce
1 cup mayonnaise
¼ cup chopped green pepper
½ teaspoon dry mustard
1 tablespoon minced onion
1 tablespoon chopped pimento
½ teaspoon horseradish
Dash hot pepper
Freshly ground black pepper to taste

## Captain's Seafood Salad

1 four and a half-ounce can crabmeat, rinsed and drained
1 four and a half-ounce can shrimp, rinsed and drained
1 onion, chopped fine
1 green pepper, chopped fine
1 cup celery, chopped
1 cup mayonnaise
1 teaspoon Worcestershire sauce
Dash pepper
Lemon wedges

Combine crab, shrimp, onion, pepper and celery. Add mayonnaise, Worcestershire sauce and pepper. Divide between six baking shells. Bake at 350 degrees for 30 minutes. Garnish with lemon wedges. Serves six.

## Shrimp A La Creme Salad

3 pounds large shrimp, boiled with shells on,
    then shelled and deveined
4 hard cooked eggs, yolks sieved and whites chopped
3 tablespoons sugar
4 tablespoons white wine vinegar
2 teaspoons Dijon-style mustard
¼ teaspoon freshly ground black pepper
2 cups mayonnaise
1 tablespoon capers, drained
2 onions, thinly sliced
¼ cup whipped cream
½ cup sour cream
Lettuce leaves

To egg yolks, add sugar, vinegar, mustard, pepper and mayonnaise. Stir in capers, chopped egg whites, onions and shrimp. Fold in whipped and sour creams. Serve in lettuce cups. Serves eight.

# Shrimp And Shells Salad

1 pound cooked, cleaned and shelled shrimp or
   4 4½-ounce cans shrimp, drained
2 cups cooked macaroni shells
½ cup chopped raw cauliflower
½ cup chopped raw broccoli flowerets
1 cup sliced celery
1 tablespoon chopped pimiento
¼ cup each sweet pickle relish and chopped parsley
½ cup mayonnaise or salad dressing
¼ cup sour cream
3 tablespoons bottled French dressing
1 tablespoon lemon juice
1 tablespoon minced onion
½ teaspoon celery seed
½ teaspoon salt
Freshly ground black pepper to taste
1 hard-cooked egg, chopped
Lettuce leaves

Combine shrimp, shells, cauliflower, broccoli, celery, relish and pimiento. In a small bowl, mix together the mayonnaise, sour cream, French dressing, lemon juice, onion, celery seed, salt and pepper. Fold into shrimp mixture to coat shrimp and vegetables well. Divide between lettuce-lined plates and garnish with the chopped egg. Serves six.

# Crab-Shrimp Salad

1 head, each leaf and romaine lettuce, torn into bite-size pieces
¾ pound shrimp, cooked and cleaned
¾ pound lump crab meat or Alaskan king crab meat in
   bite-size chunks
1 red onion, thinly sliced
½ cup radishes, thinly sliced
1 green pepper, diced
2 stalks celery, diced
½ cup black olives, pitted
4 anchovies
Roquefort or ranch-style creamy onion dressing

In large salad bowl, toss lettuce and arrange remaining ingredients over lettuce. Top with dressing and serve to four to six.

# Avocado Neptune

½ pound scallops
½ pound shrimp
½ pound crab meat
1 quart water
1 small onion, sliced
½ lemon, sliced
½ cup white wine

Combine water, onion, lemon and wine and bring to a boil. Add scallops and simmer three minutes. Remove with a slotted spoon. Add shrimp to boiling water and simmer three minutes. Cool scallops and shrimp and with crab meat add to:

2 green onions, chopped, including tops
¼ cup fresh parsley, chopped
1 cup mayonnaise
2 large avocados, peeled and cut into fourths.
Lettuce leaves
Lime juice and garlic powder

Make a dressing of the onions, parsley and mayonnaise. Fold in shellfish. Arrange avocado quarters on lettuce and sprinkle with lime juice to prevent darkening. Dust with garlic powder. Top with shellfish mixture. Serves eight.

# Creamy Dilled Shrimp on Bibb

1½ pounds shrimp, cooked and cleaned
½ cup peeled and chopped cucumber
½ cup mayonnaise
½ cup commercial sour cream
2 tablespoons minced onion
1 tablespoon dill weed
2 teaspoons lemon juice
1 clove garlic, minced
8 drops liquid hot pepper sauce
Freshly ground pepper and salt to taste
Bibb lettuce

Combine cucumber, mayonnaise, sour cream, onion, dill weed, lemon juice, garlic, hot pepper sauce, pepper and salt and mix well. Fold in shrimp and arrange over bibb lettuce. Serves six.

# Shrimp-Rice Salad

1 pound cooked, shelled and cleaned shrimp or
  3 4½-ounce cans shrimp, drained
2 cups cooked brown rice
½ cup chopped fresh parsley
¾ cup thinly sliced celery
¼ cup sliced ripe olives
½ cup mayonnaise or salad dressing
2 tablespoons each bottled French dressing and
  fresh lemon juice
½ teaspoon curry powder
Lettuce leaves

If shrimp are large, cut in half. Combine rice parsley, celery, olives and shrimp. Mix mayonnaise with French dressing and lemon juice. Add curry powder, mixing until smooth. Fold into shrimp mixture and mound on lettuce leaves. Serves six.

# Shrimp In Tomato Aspic Ring

1 pound shrimp, cooked, shelled and cleaned
2 tablespoons gelatin
2 cups tomato juice
2 teaspoons grated fresh onion
2 tablespoons chopped sweet pickles
1 tablespoon fresh lemon juice
2 teaspoons horseradish
¼ teaspoon salt
Dash freshly ground black pepper
Lettuce leaves
Mayonnaise or salad dressing

If shrimp are large, cut in half lengthwise. Soften the gelatin in ½ cup of the tomato juice for five minutes. Scald the 1½ cups remaining tomato juice and stir into gelatin until gelatin is dissolved. Add the next six ingredients and then stir in shrimp. Turn into a ring mold and chill until firm. Unmold onto a bed of lettuce leaves and garnish with mayonnaise. Serves six.

*Shrimp and pasta — it's a new combination, but one that is catching on fast as we look for light meals. This shrimp and "rotelle" or corkscrew pasta salad has everything. A delicious first course, it can go it alone with buttered and toasted garlic bread for a nutritious light dinner.*

## Shrimp And Pasta Salad

1 pound small raw shrimp, shelled and cleaned
2 cups thinly sliced zucchini
2 cups sliced fresh mushrooms
1 cup small green beans, cut into one-inch lengths
2 tablespoons salad oil
8 ounces rotelle or corkscrew pasta, cooked according to
    package directions
2 tablespoons lemon juice
1 clove garlic, minced
1 medium onion, thinly sliced and separated into rings
¾ cup Italian dressing, bottled or homemade

Saute zucchini, mushrooms and green beans in salad oil until they begin to soften slightly. Remove with a slotted spoon and add shrimp to pan, along with lemon juice, garlic and onion. Saute until shrimp turn pink and are done. Remove to bowl of vegetables. Add pasta and dressing, tossing gently to coat. Refrigerate until chilled through. Serve over lettuce leaves. Serves eight.

## Marinated Shrimp Salad

4 cups cooked and cleaned shrimp
¼ teaspoon paprika
Bottled or homemade French dressing
⅓ cup mayonnaise
16 small sweet pickles
Shredded lettuce

Sprinkle paprika over shrimp and then cover with French dressing. Chill and marinate at least one hour. Stir in mayonnaise and arrange shrimp over lettuce, on eight plates. Garnish with pickles. Serves eight.

*The addition of fresh fruits to shrimp salads is a stroke of genius — as the next five recipes will prove.*

## Orange Shrimp

1 ½ pounds shrimp, cooked, shelled and cleaned
2 large oranges, peeled and sliced into wheels
1 small onion, sliced and separated into rings
⅓ cup cider vinegar
⅓ cup fresh lemon juice
¼ cup sugar
1 cup vegetable oil
1 tablespoons paprika
2 teaspoons dry mustard
2 cloves garlic, minced
½ teaspoon salt
¼ teaspoon crushed red chilies, optional

Layer cooled shrimp with oranges and onion rings in a glass or ceramic serving container. Combine the remaining ingredients, shaking well. Pour over the shrimp. Cover and refrigerate at least one hour to blend flavors. Serves four to six.

## Spinach-Orange Shrimp Salad

1 pound shrimp, cooked and shelled
3 large oranges, sectioned
1 medium red onion, thinly sliced
½ pound fresh spinach, torn into bite-size pieces
¾ cup olive oil
¼ cup fresh lemon juice
1 teaspoon each sugar and prepared Dijon mustard
Salt and pepper to taste

In a large bowl or on large serving platter, make bed of spinach. Arrange shrimp, orange sections and onions. Make a dressing of the olive oil, lemon juice, sugar, mustard and salt and pepper. Pour over chilled salad. Serves four.

# Tropical Shrimp Salad

1 ½ pounds shrimp in the shell, raw
2 tablespoons salad oil
1 teaspoon ground ginger
½ teaspoon curry powder
2 cloves garlic, minced
½ cup salad oil
2 tablespoons rum
¼ cup fresh lime juice
1 tablespoon Dijon-style mustard
¼ teaspoon salt
Dash of bottled hot pepper sauce
2 medium papayas, peeled and seeded
3 kiwi fruits, sliced or one cup strawberries, sliced
1 eight-ounce can sliced pineapple, drained
Lime wedges

Saute shrimp in the two tablespoons of the oil until they turn pink. Drain and cool shrimp on paper toweling while you heat in the same skillet the ginger, curry powder, garlic and one-half cup of oil. Simmer three minutes. Remove from heat and cool. Shell and devein shrimp and place in a glass shallow dish. To oil mixture in skillet, add the rum, lime juice, mustard, salt and hot pepper sauce. Whisk in one tablespoon of the soft papaya, scraped from the center. Pour into blender or bowl of food processor and process until smooth and creamy. Pour this dressing over the shrimp. Cover and marinate at least two hours. Remove shrimp with a slotted spoon and place on serving platter. Slice the papaya and arrange with the sliced kiwi fruits and pineapple. Spoon some of the reserved dressing over this. Garnish with lime wedges. Serves four.

# Islander Shrimp Salad

1 4 ½ -ounce can shrimp, drained
2 medium bananas, sliced
2 tomatoes cut in wedges
1 small can mandarin orange sections, drained
1 cup seedless green grapes
Sliced ripe olives for garnish
2 tablespoons salad oil
2 tablespoons cider vinegar or wine vinegar
⅛ teaspoon freshly ground black pepper
1 teaspoon honey
2 tablespoons grated onion

Combine shrimp and fruits in serving bowl. Mix salad oil, vinegar, pepper, honey and onion and pour this dressing over contents of salad bowl. Garnish with ripe olive slices. Serves four.

## Jeweled Shrimp Medley

¾ pound cooked, shelled and cleaned medium to large shrimp
1 large seedless orange, peeled, sliced and cut in quarters
1 cup purple grapes, sliced in half and seeded
1 small can white asparagus tips
Leaf lettuce
¼ cup mayonnaise
¼ cup sour cream
1 teaspoon bottled chili sauce
1 tablespoon lemon juice
⅛ teaspoon Worcestershire sauce
1 teaspoon grated horseradish
Garnishes of four cooked crab claws, whole purple grapes
    and orange slices

Line the bottoms of four stemmed glasses with lettuce leaves and fill with a combination of orange sections, grape halves, shrimp and asparagus spears. Combine the mayonnaise, sour cream, chili sauce, lemon juice, Worcestershire sauce and horseradish. Mix until smooth and pour dressing over shrimp mixture. Garnish each glass with a crab claw, orange slices and grapes. Serves four.

## Shrimp-Cheese Salad Bowl

1 pound, cooked, shelled and cleaned medium to large shrimp
1 cup mild Cheddar cheese, grated
2 tomatoes, cut in bite-sized pieces
1½ quarts leaf lettuce
¼ cup sliced green onions, including tops
½ cup sliced ripe olives
1 cup sliced cucumber
¾ cup creamy Italian salad dressing

Arrange shrimp, Cheddar cheese, tomatoes, lettuce, onions, olives and cucumber in large salad bowl. Top with homemade or purchased salad dressing. Serves six.

# Shrimp Salad (Filling) I

2 cups cooked, cleaned and shelled shrimp
½ cup chopped celery
½ cup toasted slivered almonds
½ teaspoon celery salt
¼ teaspoon white pepper
2 tablespoons lemon juice
½ cup salad dressing or mayonnaise

Combine all ingredients and serve well chilled on lettuce leaves or in halves of scooped out cantaloupes or pineapple quarters. This can also be used as a sandwich filling. Serves six.

# Shrimp Salad (Filling) II

1 pound cooked, shelled and cleaned shrimp, cut in half if large
1 hard boiled egg, chopped
½ cup mayonnaise or salad dressing
1 tablespoon sweet pickle relish
2 tablespoons minced onion
2 tablespoons finely chopped green pepper
Dash of bottled hot pepper sauce
Salt and pepper to taste

Combine shrimp with next five ingredients, mixing lightly. Add hot pepper sauce and season with salt and pepper. Serve on leaf lettuce or as a sandwich filling. Serves four.

# Shrimp Oriental

1 ½ pounds small shrimp, cooked, shelled and cleaned
½ pound fresh mushrooms, sliced
1 cup fresh bean sprouts
1 cup fresh alfalfa sprouts
4 green onions sliced, tops included
1 small green (or red) pepper, thinly sliced
1 eight-ounce can sliced water chestnuts, drained
¼ cup bottled teriyaki sauce
3 tablespoons sesame seed oil or vegetable oil
2 tablespoons rice wine vinegar or wine vinegar
½ teaspoon ground ginger
1 teaspoon sesame seeds for garnish
Leaf lettuce

Combine first seven ingredients. Mix together the teriyaki sauce, oil, vinegar and ginger. Pour over shrimp mixture and toss well. Cover and refrigerate two hours or until chilled. Arrange lettuce on four plates. Mound shrimp mixture on top of lettuce. Sprinkle each with some of the sesame seeds and serve. Serves four.

# Spring Shrimp

2 cups cooked, shelled, cleaned shrimp
¼ cup each wine vinegar and vegetable oil
2 tablespoons sugar
¼ cup long grain rice
2 cups boiling water
¼ teaspoon salt
1 cup fresh pea pods, bias-sliced in one-inch pieces,
   uncooked
1 green onion, bias sliced
Fresh spinach
¼ cup toasted sliced almonds

Put shrimp in a small bowl. Combine vinegar, oil and sugar and pour over shrimp. Chill and marinate at least four hours. Cook rice in the two cups boiling water with the salt, 15 minutes. Remove from heat and cool slightly. Stir in pea pods, and onion. Chill. Drain shrimp, reserving marinade. Arrange spinach on four salad plates. Top with rice mixture and pour marinade over rice. Circle rice with the shrimp and garnish with almonds. Serves four.

# Shrimp In Cheese Tarts

2 cups cooked, cleaned and shelled shrimp, chopped
¾ cup chopped celery
¼ cup finely chopped green onions, including tops
1 medium apple, unpeeled and chopped
1 cup seedless green grapes, halved
½ cup coarsely chopped pecans
¼ cup each sour cream and mayonnaise
4 teaspoons lemon juice
⅛ teaspoon dry mustard
Cheese tart shells, recipe follows

In a medium bowl, combine shrimp, celery, onions, apple, grapes and pecans. In a small bowl, mix until smooth, the sour cream and mayonnaise, lemon juice, and mustard. Fold into shrimp mixture. Serve, well chilled, in tart shells. Serves five.

### Cheese Tart Shells

2 cups sifted all-purpose flour
1 teaspoon salt
½ cup salad oil
1 cup grated Cheddar cheese
3 tablespoons cold water

Combine flour and salt. Stir in salad oil with a fork or pastry blender and then stir in cheese until the mixture resembles coarse crumbs. Stir in water, gathering dough to a ball. Roll half of the dough between pieces of wax paper and cut in circles to fit tart or muffin cup pans. Bake at 425 degrees about 12 minutes, or until lightly browned. Remove from pans to cool. Dough can be fitted on outsides of tart pans or custard cups for baking and easy removal when done.

# Hot Shrimp Risotto Salad

½ pound cooked, shelled and cleaned shrimp, sliced
2 cups cooked rice
2 tablespoons bottled chili sauce
2 tablespoons vinegar
1 teaspoon sugar
1 tablespoon horseradish
¼ cup salad oil
2 tablespoons chopped parsley and toasted almonds for garnish

In a saucepan, combine the chili sauce, vinegar, sugar, horseradish and salad oil. Heat through, mixing well. Add shrimp pieces and rice to saucepan and heat through again, stirring occasionally. Sprinkle with parsley and almonds and serve at once with nacho corn chips.

## South Of The Border Shrimp Salad

1 ½ pounds cooked, shelled and cleaned shrimp
2 cups guacamole dip, recipe follows
1 tablespoon each lemon juice and Worcestershire sauce
½ teaspoon each garlic powder, hot pepper sauce
⅛ teaspoon crushed red chilies
6 corn tortillas, fried in a potato nest basket or fried flat
Shredded lettuce and chopped tomato for garnish

Combine the guacamole dip, lemon juice, Worcestershire sauce, garlic powder and hot pepper sauce and chilies. Chill. Fill bottoms of tortilla "cups" with some of the lettuce and about ⅓ cup of guacamole mixture. Garnish top with more lettuce and tomato, setting each tortilla on a bed of lettuce leaves. Arrange shrimp around each. Serves six.

## Guacamole Dip

2 fully ripe avocados, peeled, seed removed
2 tablespoons chopped onion
3 tablespoons lemon juice
3 tablespoons mayonnaise
½ teaspoon paprika

Process until smooth in a food processor or blender. Makes about two cups.

# Curried Shrimp Salad For Two

1 four and a half-ounce can shrimp, rinsed and drained
½ cup mayonnaise
1 tablespoon soy sauce
1 teaspoon lemon juice
½ cup fresh bean sprouts
1 teaspoon curry powder
½ cup chopped celery
Lettuce leaves

Combine first seven ingredients. Chill and serve on lettuce leaves. Serves two.

# Sandwiches

*Not exactly a sandwich, these crispy little turnovers can still be eaten out-of hand and are delicious served with a tossed or fruit salad for a light lunch.*

## Shrimp Turnovers

½ pound cooked, shelled and cleaned shrimp
¼ cup mayonnaise or salad dressing
1 tablespoon lemon juice
1 teaspoon horseradish
1 tablespoon sweet pickle relish, drained
1 teaspoon prepared mustard
Pastry for one nine-inch piecrust
Milk to brush on pastry

Grind shrimp and combine the rest of the ingredients, except the pastry and milk. Roll pastry thin and cut into five-inch circles. Place a couple tablespoons of the shrimp mixture on each circle. Brush edges of pastry with milk and fold over, pressing edges together with a fork. Brush tops with more milk and cut steam vents or prick tops. Bake at 400 degrees on a lightly greased baking sheet, about 12 to 15 minutes or until lightly browned. Serves four to six.

## Creamed Shrimp On Toast

1 pound shrimp, cooked, shelled and cleaned, reserve liquid
   from cooking
2 tablespoons butter or margarine
3 green onions, chopped, including tops
2 tablespoons all-purpose flour
1 cup commercial sour cream
Salt and pepper to taste

Dredge the shrimp with the flour and along with the onions, cook in the butter about five minutes, without browning the onions. Add about one-quarter cup of the water left from boiling the shrimp to the pan and then stir in sour cream. Simmer until thickened and heated through. Season to taste with the salt and pepper. Serve on buttered toast. Serves four.

# Egg Shrimpwich

3 hard boiled eggs, coarsely chopped
½ cup chopped walnuts
1 cup cooked, shelled and deveined shrimp
½ cup mayonnaise
2 cups alfalfa sprouts or lettuce leaves
4 pita breads

Combine chopped eggs, nuts, shrimp and fold in mayonnaise. Divide alfalfa sprouts between the four pita breads and stuff each with sandwich filling. Serves four.

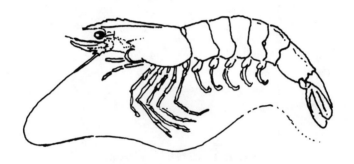

# Toasted Shrimp Sandwich With Cheese

2 cups Cheddar cheese, grated
4 tablespoons butter or margarine
¼ cup minced onion
2 tablespoons lemon juice
1 tablespoon Worcestershire sauce
½ teaspoon paprika
Freshly ground black pepper to taste
1 pound shrimp, cooked, shelled and deveined, cut up
12 hotdog rolls, split and lightly buttered

Combine cheese, butter and onion (works well in food processor) and stir in lemon juice, Worcestershire sauce, paprika and pepper. Fold in coarsely chopped shrimp. Fill rolls with shrimp mixture, leaving slightly spread. Broil about four inches from heat until bubbly and lightly browned (three to five minutes). Serves 12.

# Shrimp Salad in Croissants

1 cup cooked, cleaned and shelled shrimp (may use canned shrimp)
2 cups shredded leaf lettuce, not iceberg
1 medium carrot, shredded
4 large radishes, unpeeled and shredded
1 cup fresh alfalfa sprouts
2 green onions, sliced, tops included
¼ cup chopped walnuts
⅓ cup bottled creamy cucumber dressing, more if necessary
4 croissants, split lengthwise

Combine first seven ingredients and spoon onto bottom halves of croissants (they may be pre-heated if desired). Top each with some of the dressing and cover with other half of croissants. Serves four.

*I just want my readers to know that typing (yes, I type on a manual typewriter. I may have a food processor, but I'm still enough of a traditionalist not to have a word processor!) this recipe section of this book has been agony. My stomach grumbles, rumbles and complains. My mouth salivates and I've had to nail my shirt tail to the chair to keep me from jumping up and heading for the kitchen. It's been rough to this point, but it doesn't promise to be any better. Right now I could go for one of these:*

# Italian Shrimp Bagels

1 cup shrimp, cooked and shelled or one small can shrimp
1 cup shredded mozzarella cheese
¼ cup chopped green onions, tops included
¼ teaspoon garlic powder
1 tablespoon butter or margarine
2 tablespoons chopped fresh parsley
1 tablespoon chopped fresh basil
2 bagels, split (or four 1½-inch thick slices fresh Italian bread)

Sprinkle the cheese, dividing it evenly over the four halves of the bagels. Broil until cheese is melted and bubbly, about three minutes. In the meantime, saute the shrimp with the green onion, garlic powder, parsley and basil in the butter, just until the onions become tender. Divide this mixture between the four bagel halves. Serves four.

*What would you call a Chinese egg roll? Well, besides delicious, I call it a sandwich — at least a type of a sandwich. Add shrimp to egg rolls and you can call them divine.*

# Shrimp Egg Rolls

2 cups shredded Chinese cabbage or Romaine lettuce
1 clove garlic, minced
1 large onion, chopped
½ cup each chopped snow peas and drained canned
    water chestnuts
2 cups fresh bean sprouts
2 tablespoons sesame seed oil or vegetable oil
2 cups cooked, shelled, cleaned and chopped shrimp
1 egg, slightly beaten
2 tablespoons dry sherry
1 tablespoon soy sauce
⅛ teaspoon cayenne pepper
10 egg roll wrappers (found in produce sections or refrigerated
    food sections of supermarkets)
Sweet and sour dipping sauce, optional
Hot mustard sauce for dipping, optional

In a large skillet, saute the garlic and onion in two teaspoons of the oil. Add Chinese cabbage, snow peas, water chestnuts and bean sprouts. Stir fry about three minutes. Cover and steam one minute. In a large bowl, combine vegetables, shrimp, beaten egg, sherry, soy sauce and pepper.

Spoon one half cup of the filling evenly down the center of each egg roll wrapper. Fold one long side of wrapper over the top and around filling. Fold in both ends, using fingers to compress filling into wrapper. Fold remaining side up and over the top and ends. Brush roll with about one-half teaspoon sesame seed oil. Repeat with remaining filling and wrappers. Place rolls, seam side down on baking sheet so that they aren't touching.

Bake at 350 degrees for 15 minutes or until golden brown. Serve with sweet and sour sauce and mustard sauce if desired. Makes 10 shrimp egg rolls.

# Shrimp-Sausage Burgers

½ pound shrimp, raw, but shelled
½ pound hot bulk pork sausage
½ cup chopped green onions, tops included
1 clove garlic minced
2 tablespoons salad oil
Hamburger rolls

In food processor, grind raw shrimp. Add sausage, onions and garlic and process until mixture is smooth, only a few seconds. Make six patties and add patties to oil in a skillet. Fry until cooked through and golden on the outside. Serve on hamburger rolls, with lettuce, relish and mustard. Serves six.

# Upside Down Shrimp Sandwiches

1 cup shrimp, cooked and cleaned or one 4½-ounce can
    shrimp drained
8 slices buttered whole wheat bread
1 cup grated Swiss cheese
3 eggs, lightly beaten
1½ cups chicken boullion or shrimp stock, see recipe under Basics
2 teaspoons Worcestershire sauce
1 tablespoon Dijon-style mustard
Dash nutmeg

Place four of the slices of bread in an eight-inch square baking dish, with buttered side down. Sprinkle half of the cheese on the bread and divide shrimp between sliced and top with remaining cheese. Cover with remaining slices, buttered side up. Whisk together the eggs, broth, Worcestershire sauce and nutmeg. Pour over bread. Bake about 40 minutes at 350 degrees. Serves four.

# Main Dishes

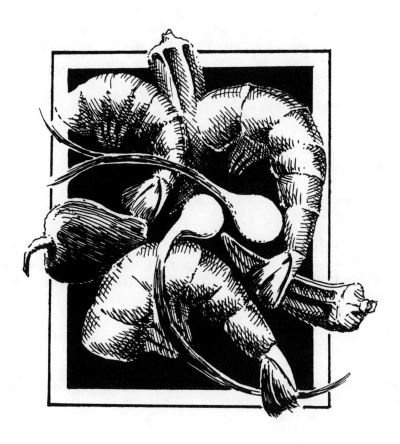

As you may have already noticed, most, if not all of the recipes so far have had little or no salt added. This is for more than one reason. In addition to the fact that most of us ingest more salt than our bodies need, salt tends to toughen many meats and seafoods — especially shrimp. It also overwhelms the delicate flavors in many dishes. Those dishes containing tomatoes or tomato products are naturally salty and rarely need any additional salt. Instead, I've added herbs and spices to enhance the flavors of the fresh seafoods and vegetables. It's all part of a lighter and healthier approach to cooking that doesn't have to rely on those health food gimmicks like soy pastes, unprocessed bran and such. What could be healthier and more natural than fresh vegetables and seafoods? If you are used to eating plenty of salt on your foods, cutting down will take some getting used to. But you'll see it will be well worth the effort; not only will you be eating healthier, but you will be enjoying it more.

I'll start out this section with what is probably one of the most popular ways to serve shrimp — fried. Granted, it's not the only way to serve shrimp, but these versions are tried and true.

## Breaded Fried Shrimp

1 ½ pounds shrimp, medium to large, shelled and deveined
2 eggs, beaten
½ cup each all-purpose flour and dry bread crumbs
¼ teaspoon pepper
Fat for deep frying

Combine eggs, flour and pepper. Dip each shrimp in this mixture and then roll in crumbs. Fry in a deep-frying basket at 350 degrees for two to three minutes, or until golden brown and cooked through. Drain on paper toweling. Serves four.

## Beer Battered Fried Shrimp

2 pounds shrimp, shelled, leaving tails on and deveined
1 cup beer, warm or cold, flat or active
1 cup all-purpose flour
Hot fat for deep frying

At least three hours before cooking, combine the beer and flour. Cover and let sit at room temperature. When ready to cook, whisk batter to re-mix and dip dry shrimp in batter, letting excess drip off. Fry in deep fat, 350 degrees, for two to three minutes, or until golden and cooked through. Drain on paper toweling. Serves four.

*Here's yet another version of fried shrimp, this one calling on coconut to add a delightful difference. A similar dish was served at a White House wedding a few years ago, causing quite a stir and creating an instant food craze.*

## Coconut Island Shrimp

2 pounds shrimp, large to jumbo, shelled, butterflied,
    leave tails on
1 ½ cups packaged pancake mix
1 cup milk
1 egg
1 ½ teaspoons curry powder
1 tablespoon vegetable oil
3 cups toasted shredded coconut
Hot fat for deep frying

Beat together the pancake mix, milk, egg, curry powder and oil. Dip each shrimp in the batter, letting excess drip off. Then roll each shrimp in the coconut and fry in deep fat at 350 degrees, two to three minutes or until golden and cooked through. Drain on paper toweling. Serves four.

*Eggplant, which has the nickname of "oyster plant," is a natural to pair with shrimp. Here are two ways to accomplish that marriage of flavors.*

## Shrimp and Eggplant

2 pounds shrimp, peeled and deveined
1 large eggplant, boiled whole
1 cup chopped celery
1 cup chopped green onion, tops included
½ cup butter or margarine
¼ teaspoon bottled hot pepper sauce
Freshly ground pepper
¼ cup chopped parsley
1 teaspoon chopped basil

Peel eggplant and cut in one-half inch cubes. Saute the celery, and onions in the butter. Add eggplant and heat through. Then stir in remaining ingredients and shrimp and simmer 10 minutes, or until shrimp is done. Serves six.

# Uptown Eggplant

1 medium-large eggplant, quartered, unpeeled
1 quart boiling water
1 tablespoon vinegar
2 slices bacon, chopped and fried until crisp
1 cup chopped green onion, tops included
1 4½-ounce can shrimp, drained
Paprika

Boil the quartered eggplant in the one-quart of water, with the vinegar until eggplant is soft, but not mushy. Drain, peel eggplant and chop. In some of the bacon grease, saute the green onion. Add the eggplant and shrimp. Turn into a greased casserole and sprinkle with the bacon. Bake at 350 degrees for 25 minutes, or until heated through and flavors blended. Serves four.

*It may be spelled "pilau," but in the South this traditional dish is called "pur'-low" and shows up at many a community dinner and fund raiser. An easy-going dish, it can be made in large batches calling on anything from chicken to ham to sausage to shrimp. Of course, here we'll go with shrimp:*

# Shrimp Pilau

1 pound shrimp, shelled and deveined
½ cup thick-sliced bacon, diced
1 cup onion, chopped
1 cup green pepper, chopped
1 cup celery, chopped
1 one-pound can whole tomatoes, chopped, liquid reserved
1 cup water
1 cup long-grain rice
¼ teaspoon thyme
¼ teaspoon sugar
Salt and pepper to taste

If shrimp are large, cut in half. In a three-quart or larger pan, saute bacon until crisp. Remove bacon and in some of the fat, cook onion, green pepper and celery until tender. Add tomatoes to vegetables, along with tomato liquid. Stir in water and rice and bring to a boil. Add thyme and sugar and reduce heat. Cover and cook until rice is done, about 20 minutes. Mix in shrimp and cook another 15 to 20 minutes, or until shrimp are done. Garnish with the bacon. Serves six.

*Another Southern tradition is the shrimp boil. Usually this is accomplished in beer, that is the shrimp are cooked in beer, along with other seafoods, sometimes potatoes and corn on the cob. The meal is often spread on newspapers and diners roll up their sleeves and enjoy the feast along with icy cold beer to wash it all down. The following recipe also includes blue crabs and serves a crowd.*

## Southern Seafood Boil

¼ cup salt
Hot water
20 small onions, peeled
12 medium potatoes, scrubbed, unpeeled
3 bulbs of garlic
1 three-ounce package crab boil
1 cup vinegar
5 lemons, halved
3 dozen live blue crabs
12 ears corn, halved
6 pounds large shrimp, unpeeled, heads on if desired.

Fill a six-gallon pot, two-thirds full of water and add salt. Bring to a boil and add potatoes and onions. Cover and cook over high heat about 20 minutes or until potatoes are almost done. Stir in crab boil, crabs, garlic, vinegar and lemons. Reduce heat, cover and simmer 10 minutes. Add corn and simmer five minutes more. Add shrimp and let stand five minutes. Drain water and arrange vegetables and seafoods on a platter. Serve with melted butter and cocktail sauce. Serves eight to 12.

## Shrimp-Rice Casserole

2 pounds shrimp, shelled and deveined
½ cup chopped onion
¼ cup vegetable oil
2 teaspoons Worcestershire sauce
4 cups cooked rice
4 slices bacon
Cayenne pepper and salt to taste

Saute the onion and shrimp in a skillet until onions are soft, about five minutes. Stir in Worcestershire sauce and rice and turn into a one and one-half quart casserole. Season with cayenne pepper and top with strips of bacon. Bake at 375 degrees about 25 minutes, or until bacon is crisp. Serves six.

*The following recipe is rich due to the addition of heavy cream. Legend has it that the recipe was named for a rather modest bon vivant by the name of Wenburg who scrambled his name to escape notoriety when naming this famous dish.*

## Shrimp Newberg

**1 pound shrimp, cooked, shelled and deveined**
**¼ cup butter or margarine, melted**
**3 tablespoons dry sherry**
**1½ cups heavy cream**
**2 egg yolks, beaten**
**Salt and cayenne pepper to taste**

Saute the shrimp slightly in the butter. Stir in sherry and heavy cream and stir a little of this mixture into the egg yolks. Add to shrimp mixture, stirring constantly and cooking over low heat until thickened. Season with salt and cayenne. Serve on toast points. Serves four to six.

*At a picturesque eaterie on Georgia's St. Simons Island, one of the house specialties is a delicious concoction called Shrimp and Green Noodles. The green noodles, of course, are spinach fettuccine which can be purchased in the super-market or made at home. The following is my close approximation of this colorful little casserole that is served in personal ramekins.*

## Shrimp With Green Noodles

**Shrimp Newberg, prepared according to previous recipe**
**6 ounces spinach fettuccine, broken and prepared according to package directions**
**1 cup sliced fresh mushrooms**
**2 tablespoons butter or margarine**
**1 cup grated Parmesan cheese, preferably freshly grated**

Saute the mushrooms in the butter and fold into the Shrimp Newberg along with the spinach noodles. Divide this mixture between four individual casseroles and top with the cheese. Bake 20 minutes at 350 degrees until hot and bubbly. If desired, broil briefly to brown cheese on top. Serves four.

# Curried Shrimp With Coconut

¼ cup butter or margarine
2 cloves garlic, minced
1 medium onion, chopped
1 mango, peeled and cubed
2 tablespoons lime juice
1 cup coconut milk
2 teaspoons curry powder
¼ teaspoon white pepper
2 pounds shrimp, peeled and deveined
Hot cooked rice
1 cup freshly grated coconut

In the butter, saute the garlic and onion. Add mango and simmer about five minutes. Stir in lime juice, coconut milk, curry powder and pepper. Simmer 10 minutes, uncovered. Stir in shrimp and cook 10 to 15 minutes, or until shrimp are done. Serve over the hot rice, garnished with the fresh coconut. Serves four to six.

*One potato, two potato ... take a potato and stuff it with something hearty and you have your entree. How about a tangy shrimp and cheese mixture?*

# Potatoes Stuffed With Shrimp

1 pound shrimp, cooked, shelled and deveined —
  halved if large
4 large potatoes, baked
½ cup butter or margarine
¼ cup chopped green onion, tops included
½ cup sour cream
1 cup Cheddar cheese, shredded
Paprika
Chopped parsley

Halve potatoes and scoop out pulp, leaving a one-quarter inch thick shell. Combine the potato pulp, the butter, green onion, cream, cheese and stir in shrimp. Stuff the potato shells with this mixture. Top with paprika. Bake at 425 degrees for 15 minutes or until heated through and golden on top. Garnish with fresh parsley. Serves four.

*Devised to be fuel efficient, the Chinese method of stir-frying is quick and helps preserve the fresh color, texture and flavor of foods. For seafood, stir-frying is perfect. The key to success with Chinese recipes is to have everything ready before you start to cook. Dice or chop those vegetables, measure and have everything at hand because most steps in this method only take a minute or two — no time to search for an ingredient or measuring spoon. I'll start out with my version of Shrimp Fried Rice. I've tried a lot of cookbook recipes for fried rice, but they just never seem to match the results of Chinese restaurants. The following recipe comes as close as possible — in looks and taste.*

## Shrimp Fried Rice

1 cup or one 4½-ounce can small shrimp,
  shelled and cleaned
1 egg beaten with two tablespoons water
3 cups fresh bean sprouts
1 cup sliced green onion, tops included
1½ teaspoons honey
¼ teaspoon garlic powder
3 tablespoons soy sauce
3 cups cold cooked, long-grain rice
½ teaspoon ground ginger
Vegetable oil or sesame seed oil for stir frying

Drain shrimp and pat dry. Set aside. In a small skillet, scramble egg over medium heat, until cooked. Set aside. In a wok or large skillet, heat about two tablespoons of the oil and stir fry the onions and bean sprouts about two minutes. Cover and steam about one minute, until bright green and slightly tender, but not limp. Remove vegetables from skillet.

Stir soy sauce into the rice so that it is absorbed evenly. Set aside. To the skillet, add more oil if necessary and over high heat, stir fry shrimp about one-half minute. Drizzle honey over shrimp and stir fry another half minute to glaze shrimp. Sprinkle shrimp with garlic powder. Remove shrimp from pan. Add rice to skillet and stir in vegetables. Stir fry about a minute over medium-high heat to heat through. Stir in shrimp and then just before serving, stir in scrambled egg. Serves four.

## Sweet-Sour Shrimp

1 pound shrimp, shelled and deveined
1 cup chopped green onions, including tops
½ cup each chopped green and sweet red pepper
2 cups fresh bean sprouts

2 rings pineapple, cut in one-half inch chunks
2 tablespoons vegetable oil
1 clove garlic, minced
2 cups chicken bouillon, can be made from
  bouillon cubes
2 tablespoons vinegar
1 tablespoon catsup
1 tablespoon brown sugar
2 tablespoons corn starch mixed with two tablespoons water
½ teaspoon each cayenne and black pepper
3 cups hot cooked rice

In a large skillet or wok, heat the vegetable oil and stir fry the green onion, peppers, bean sprouts and garlic two to three minutes over medium-high heat. Stir in pineapple and add bouillon, vinegar, catsup, brown sugar and corn starch paste. Stir and cook until thickened and smooth. Stir in shrimp and cover and continue to cook three to five minutes over medium heat, or until shrimp and vegetables are done. Season to taste with pepper. Serve over hot rice. Serves four.

## Stir-Fried Shrimp With Vegetables

1 pound shrimp, uncooked, but shelled and deveined
1 teaspoon ground ginger
1 tablespoon cornstarch
2 cups fresh sliced Chinese cabbage
2 cups fresh snow pea pods
1 clove garlic, minced
3 green onions, sliced, tops included
4 tablespoons sesame seed oil or vegetable oil
1 teaspoon honey
2 tablespoons dry sherry
1 tablespoon soy sauce
2 tablespoons water
½ cup toasted sliced almonds for garnish

Combine ginger and cornstarch and coat shrimp. Have vegetables chopped, sliced, etc., and set aside. Heat oil in wok or large skillet. Add shrimp and stir fry about two to three minutes, or until shrimp cook and turn pink. Remove shrimp and add vegetables to pan. Add more oil if necessary. Stir fry vegetables three minutes over medium-high heat, until still crisp and bright-colored. Combine honey, sherry, soy sauce and water and add to skillet, stirring to combine. Cover and steam one minute. Return shrimp to pan and heat through. Garnish with toasted almonds. Serves four.

# Chinese Shrimp

1 pound shrimp, shelled and deveined
3 tablespoons dry sherry, divided
1 teaspoon gingerroot, peeled and minced
½ cup unsalted roasted cashew nuts
½ cup fresh sliced mushrooms
3 tablespoons sesame seed oil
½ cup green onions, diagonally sliced, tops included
½ cup sliced water chestnuts
2 tablespoons soy sauce
1 teaspoon cornstarch
½ teaspoon honey

Combine the shrimp, one tablespoon of the sherry and the ginger-root. Let marinate for about 30 minutes. In a wok or heavy skillet, heat the oil over medium-high heat. Stir-fry the cashew nuts in the oil for about one half minute or until golden. Drain on paper toweling. Reduce heat and add mushrooms and onions. Stir fry about one minute. Add chestnuts and shrimp mixture and stir-fry over medium-high heat about three minutes or until the shrimp are pink and done. In a small bowl, combine the remaining two tablespoons sherry, the soy sauce, cornstarch and honey and add to pan, stir-frying until this sauce is thickened and smooth, about two minutes. Top with the cashew nuts. Serves four.

# Cantonese Sweet-Sour Shrimp

1 pound shrimp, raw but shelled and deveined
4 tablespoons each all-purpose flour and cornstarch
2 tablespoons water
1 large egg, slightly beaten
Hot oil for shallow frying heated to 375 degrees
½ cup each rice wine vinegar, brown sugar and
    pineapple juice
4 slices canned pineapple, cut in chunks
2 fresh tomatoes, peeled and cut in eighths
1 green pepper, cut in strips
1 cup fresh snow pea pods
2 tablespoons vegetable oil
2 tablespoons cornstarch mixed with:
¼ cup cold water
½ cup toasted, shredded coconut for garnish

Pat shrimp dry. Combine flour, cornstarch, water and egg. Dip shrimp in this batter and fry in oil about three to five minutes, or until golden brown and cooked through. Drain on paper toweling and keep warm in a low oven while preparing the remainder of the dish.

Combine vinegar, brown sugar and pineapple juice. Set aside. In a wok or heavy skillet, heat oil. Add snow peas and green pepper and stir fry two minutes. Add tomato wedges and pineapple. Stir in vinegar mixture and then mixture of cornstarch and water. Heat, stirring, until thickened and smooth. Stir in shrimp to glaze with sauce and serve garnished with coconut. Serves four. If desired serve with cellophane noodles.

*In some areas shrimp are called scampi, which of course makes the name of the dish Shrimp Scampi redundant. But it still tastes fantastic and no selection of shrimp recipes would be complete without it. Here's mine:*

## *Shrimp Scampi*

**2 pounds large shrimp, uncooked, shelled or with shells on**
**¼ cup extra virgin olive oil**
**¼ cup butter**
**3 cloves garlic, crushed**
**2 tablespoons fresh chopped basil**
**¼ cup lemon juice**
**Freshly ground black pepper**

Depending on how messy you want to get, you can either shell the shrimp before you cook them, or not. If you leave the shells on, the shrimp will not shrink as much, have a better color and … yeah, yeah, you've heard all this before.

Heat the oil and butter in a large skillet, one large enough so shrimp won't be crowded as you cook them, or cook them in two batches. Add the garlic and basil and saute about one minute. Add shrimp and cook over medium-high heat three to five minutes, or until shrimp turn pink and are cooked. Stir in lemon juice. Serves four.

# Shrimp Marinara

1 pound shrimp, uncooked, but shelled and deveined
2 tablespoons olive oil
2 cloves garlic, minced
1 cup chopped onion
1 six-ounce can tomato paste
1 16-ounce can whole tomatoes, undrained
2 tablespoons each chopped fresh parsley and basil
1 teaspoon oregano
Hot cooked spaghetti

Saute garlic and onion in oil until soft. Add shrimp and saute two minutes, until shrimp turns pink. Break up tomatoes and add with tomato paste, parsley, oregano and basil to pan. Simmer three to five minutes, just until heated through and flavors blended. Serve over hot spaghetti. Serves four.

*As might be expected, these recipes are like a culinary romp around the globe — attesting to the fact of shrimp's universal appeal. Before we leave Italy, let's try this quick shrimp dish with a definite Italian accent.*

# Shrimp Italian

3 pounds shrimp, uncooked, leave shelr pound stick butter, no substitutions
½ cup fresh lemon juice
1 teaspoon freshly ground black pepper
¼ cup chopped fresh basil
1½ cups Italian salad dressing, bottled or homemade
Hot cooked spaghetti or crusty Italian bread

Combine the butter, lemon juice, pepper, basil and Italian salad dressing in a three-quart or larger saucepan. Bring to a boil. Add shrimp and simmer about five minutes, or until shrimp turn pink and are cooked.

Serve over hot cooked spaghetti or with Italian bread to dip up the tangy, shrimp-flavored "sauce". Serves four to six.

The quiche, while exotic fare at one time, has become a mainstay. The main dish pies can be quickly prepared if you have a pie crust in the freezer. No need to rely on store-bought frozen pie crusts. Next time you prepare pie crust, make the biggest batch and roll out a few crusts to have stashed in the freezer. After all, most of the work is in making the crust. Here are two choices, the second more a pizza than a quiche, also has a southern accent.

## Shrimp Quiche

1 unbaked 10-inch pie shell
½ pound shrimp, cooked, shelled and deveined
3 eggs
1 cup heavy cream
1 cup milk
1 cup onions, chopped
3 tablespoons butter or margarine
1 tablespoon chopped parsley
1½ cups shredded Swiss cheese
½ teaspoon onion salt, optional
Freshly ground black pepper
Nutmeg

Arrange shrimp in pie shell. Lightly beat eggs and mix in cream and milk. Saute onions in butter along with parsley. Scatter onions over shrimp. Top with shredded Swiss cheese and pour cream mixture over all. Dust with black pepper and nutmeg. Bake at 375 degrees about 45 minutes, or until quiche is golden and done. Let stand five minutes before cutting. Serves four to six.

## Cajun Quiche

1½ cups packaged biscuit mix
½ cup milk
1 tablespoon vegetable oil
1 teaspoon crumbled dried parsley and oregano
1 4½-ounce can shrimp or one cup cooked shrimp, cut up
½ cup chopped green onions, tops included
1 clove garlic minced
4 thick slices meaty bacon, fried crisp and crumbled
2 tomatoes, peeled and sliced thin
1 teaspoon fresh basil, chopped
6 ounces sliced Mozzarella cheese

Combine biscuit mix, milk, vegetable oil, parsley and oregano to form a dough. Roll out on a floured surface to fit a 10-inch pie pan. Crimp edges. Arrange shrimp over bottom of crust. In a bit of the drippings from the bacon, saute the onions and garlic. Sprinkle these over shrimp. Top with the bacon and then a layer of sliced tomatoes. Sprinkle with the basil and top with the cheese. Bake at 400 degrees for 20 to 25 minutes. Serves six.

## Shrimp and Crab Bake

1 4½-ounce can shrimp, drained
1 6-ounce can crab meat, drained
1 medium green pepper, chopped
1 medium onion, chopped
1 cup chopped celery
1 cup mayonnaise
1 tablespoon Worcestershire sauce
2 tablespoons dry sherry
Pepper to taste
1 cup buttered dry bread crumbs

Combine first nine ingredients. Layer in a two-quart casserole with crumbs, ending with crumbs on top. Bake at 350 degrees for 30 minutes. Serves four.

## Orange Poached Seafood

½ pound medium shrimp, shelled and deveined
1 pound scallops
¼ pound fresh mushrooms, sliced
1 cup snow peas, blanched
2 tablespoons orange peel
2 cups shrimp stock (see Basics recipes) or chicken broth
2 tablespoons corn starch
1 tablespoon orange flavored liqueur

Combine shrimp stock and orange peel and heat to boiling. Reduce heat to low and add shrimp, scallops and mushrooms. Cover and simmer about three minutes or until shrimp turns pink and scallops are tender. Arrange on four serving plates with snow pea pods. Keep warm.

Over medium heat, heat shrimp stock and add corn starch which has been mixed with liqueur. Stirring constantly, heat until mixture thickens and comes to a boil. Pour sauce over seafood and vegetables. Serves four.

# Creamed Shrimp on Toast

1 pound shrimp, uncooked, but shelled and deveined
¼ cup finely chopped onions
¼ cup butter or margarine
1 cup dry white wine
1 cup whipping cream
¼ teaspoon salt
Freshly ground black pepper or white pepper
Flour for dusting shrimp
Freshly chopped parsley for garnish
~~Toast points or puff pastry patty shells~~

*add cyenne pepper*
*use noodles*

Dust shrimp in the flour and saute in the butter with the onions for two to three minutes. Remove shrimp and onions from pan. Add wine, cream, salt and pepper and cook, stirring constantly, until thickened and smooth. Return shrimp and onions to pan. Heat through and serve on toast points, garnished with parsley. Serves four.


# Saucy Oven Shrimp

4 pounds shrimp, raw with shells on
½ cup butter or margarine
¼ cup lemon juice
2 cloves garlic, crushed
½ cup bottled chili sauce
½ cup extra virgin olive oil
2 tablespoons Worcestershire sauce
1 tablespoon fresh chopped parsley
1 tablespoon fresh chopped basil
1 teaspoon paprika
½ teaspoon bottled hot pepper sauce

Spread shrimp in a shallow baking pan. In a saucepan, combine remaining ingredients and bring to a boil. Reduce heat and simmer five minutes. Pour this sauce over the shrimp. Cover and marinate in the refrigerator overnight or for several hours. Bake at 360 degrees for 20 minutes, stirring twice, until shrimp are cooked. Serve shrimp with its sauce over rice or pasta or with Italian bread. Serves six to eight.

# Shrimp Melange

1 pound shrimp, uncooked, but shelled and deveined
¼ cup extra virgin olive oil
½ cup golden raisins
1 small jar marinated artichoke hearts, liquid reserved
¾ cup white asparagus tips, drained
8 ounces linuuini noodles, cooked
¼ cup lemon juice
½ cup chopped fresh parsley
¼ cup sliced, toasted almonds

Heat oil in a skillet and saute shrimp about two minutes. Add raisins and cook another minute. Add artichoke hearts and liquid, and asparagus tips. Heat through.

Toss lightly with the noodles and sprinkle with the lemon juice and parsley. Top with almonds. Serves four.

# Shrimp Croquettes

1½ pounds shrimp, cooked, shelled, deveined and chopped
1 egg
2 teaspoons butter or margarine
½ cup raw rice, cooked according to package directions
¼ teaspoon freshly ground black pepper
1 cup fine dry bread crumbs
2 eggs, slightly beaten
Hot oil for deep frying, heated to 375 degrees

Combine rice and butter. Stir in one egg, pepper and shrimp.

Shape into balls, cones or cylinders. Roll in bread crumbs, dip into beaten eggs and then coat again with the crumbs.

Deep fry for two to three minutes, or until golden brown. Avoid crowding croquettes when frying. Drain on paper toweling. Serve with a cocktail sauce made with chili sauce and mayonnaise. Makes eight to serve four.

# Over the Coals

*A natural for the barbecue grill, shrimp take on an extra dimension when cooked al fresco, over the coals. Whether you are rushing them from the trap to the dinner table via the barbecue grill or not, charcoal cooking brings out the best in this delicate shellfish. Even more important here, however, where temperatures vary and are sometimes unpredictable, is to be careful not to overcook this tender dish. Basting, frequent turning and careful timing are all important ingredients when cooking shrimp over the coals.*

## Polynesian Shrimp

1 pound shrimp, raw, shelled or unshelled
1 cup chopped green onion, tops included
2 cloves garlic, minced
1 cup fresh shredded coconut
2 tablespoons coconut milk drained from nut
1 tablespoon lemon juice
4 thick slices tomato
4 slices pineapple
Ti, banana or Swiss chard leaves or heavy duty aluminum foil
½ teaspoon each turmeric and paprika, mixed

Combine the shrimp, green onion, garlic, coconut, coconut juice, lemon juice and set aside. On a large leaf or two leaves overlapping, place a slice of tomato and top that with a slice of pineapple.

Divide the shrimp mixture between the four leaves with tomato and pineapple. Wrap, turning in ends to seal. Cook over medium coals, turning frequently, about 35 minutes. Serves four.

## Shrimp With Fruit On Skewers

1 pound shrimp, raw and unshelled
½ cup orange juice
¼ cup each vinegar and vegetable oil
3 tablespoons soy sauce
Lemon wedges
Pineapple chunks
Preserved kumquats or orange wedges

Place shrimp in a shallow glass container. Combine orange juice, vinegar, vegetable oil and soy sauce. Pour over shrimp and marinate, refrigerated, one hour. Thread shrimp on skewers, alternating with fruit. Broil over medium coals, three to four minutes, brushing often with marinade and turning frequently. Serves four.

# Quick Smoked Shrimp

2 pounds shrimp, jumbo or large, unshelled
1 cup vegetable oil
½ cup margarine, melted
1 teaspoon garlic salt

With shells on, use a sharp knife or scissors to butterfly shrimp, cutting along the back and leaving the shell attached to the underside. Remove sand vein. Place shrimp, shell side down, on grill over low coals and wet hickory chips. Brush with a mixture of the oil, margarine and garlic salt. Cook at low temperature for 10 minutes, basting several times. Turn shrimp and cook another five minutes or until shrimp are done. Serves four to six.

# Shrimp and Vegetable Packets

1 pound shrimp, shelled and deveined
8 ears fresh sweet corn, cut from cobs, about four cups
4 small zucchinis, sliced thinly
½ teaspoon sugar
½ teaspoon garlic salt
¼ teaspoon freshly ground black pepper
1 tablespoon chopped parsley
4 teaspoons lemon juice
¼ cup butter or margarine

Combine the corn and zucchini slices with the sugar, garlic salt, pepper and parsley. Divide between four squares of heavy-duty aluminum foil. Top with shrimp which has been drizzled with the lemon juice. Dot with butter. Seal packets and grill 15 to 20 minutes over medium coals. Serves four.

# South Of The Border Grilled Shrimp

1 pound large shrimp, shelled and deveined
1 cup bottled picante sauce
2 cloves garlic, minced
2 tablespoons lime juice
1 tablespoons chopped parsley

Thread shelled shrimp on skewers. Combine remaining ingredients and brush on shrimp. Grill shrimp over hot coals five to eight minutes, turning frequently and brushing with the sauce. Serve remaining sauce, hot, with shrimp. Serves four.

# Smoked Seafood Creole

1 pound shrimp, shelled and deveined
1 pint oysters, liquid reserved
¼ pound bacon, fried crisp and crumbled
2 cloves garlic, minced
1 cup each chopped onions, celery and green pepper
1 bay leaf
¼ teaspoon pepper
1 teaspoon sugar
1 one-pound can tomatoes, drained and chopped
1 cup shrimp shell stock or chicken bouillon
1 tablespoon vinegar
2 cups cut frozen okra, thawed
2 cups cooked rice
Parsley

In some of the bacon drippings, saute the garlic, onions, celery and green pepper until tender. Add the bay leaf, pepper, sugar, tomatoes, liquid from oysters, shrimp shell stock and vinegar. Simmer five minutes. Stir in okra.

Using six 10-ounce aluminum foil individual casseroles or cupped squares of heavy-duty aluminum foil, divide the rice and place vegetable mixture over. Top with shrimp and oysters. Place containers or packets on grill inside smoke oven. Smoke at 300 degrees for 15 to 20 minutes or until shrimp are done and have a golden smoke color. The edges of the oysters will curl when they are done. Garnish with chopped parsley. Serves six.

# Confetti Kebobs

1 ½ pounds shrimp, shelled and deveined
4 large carrots cut diagonally in two-inch pieces
2 green peppers cut in chunks
1 cup shrimp-shell stock or chicken bouillon
½ cup apricot preserves
¼ cup cider vinegar
2 cloves garlic, minced
½ pound fresh mushrooms
1 eight-ounce can water chestnuts, drained

Clean shrimp and set aside while parboiling carrots and green peppers just until crisp tender. In a shallow glass dish, combine the shell stock or bouillon, preserves, vinegar and garlic and toss lightly with the shrimp, carrots, peppers, mushrooms and water chestnuts. Cover and refrigerate to marinate three hours or longer. Thread shrimp, alternating with the vegetables on six skewers. Grill over medium-hot coals about five minutes, basting with marinade and turning frequently. Serves six.

# Garden Shrimp Kebobs

2 pounds large shrimp, shelled and deveined
2 medium zucchini
18 cherry tomatoes or four tomatoes cut in wedges
12 strips bacon, cooked, but still pliable
¼ cup honey
2 tablespoons soy sauce
¼ teaspoon garlic powder

Thread six long skewers with shrimp, zucchini which has been cut into one-inch chunks, tomatoes and bacon strips which have been spiraled around shrimp and vegetables as they are threaded. Combine honey, soy sauce and garlic powder and brush kebobs. Grill over medium coals about six to eight minutes, turning frequently and brushing with marinade. Serves six.

# Shrimp Kebobs

2 pounds large shrimp, shelled and deveined
1 pint cherry tomatoes or four medium tomatoes cut in wedges
2 large green peppers, cut in wedges
2 large onions, par boiled and cut in wedges
⅓ cup olive oil or vegetable oil
⅓ cup lemon juice
4 cloves garlic, minced
¼ teaspoon each salt and pepper
2 tablespoons chopped parsley

Arrange shrimp in a shallow glass container and make a marinade of the oil, lemon juice, garlic, salt, pepper and parsley. Pour over shrimp, alternating with vegetables on six 12-inch skewers. Brush with marinade and grill over medium-hot coals three to five minutes, turning frequently and brushing with marinade. Serves six.

# Lime-Buttered Shrimp

2 pounds shrimp, shelled and deveined
4 cloves garlic, minced
¼ cup fresh lime juice
½ cup butter or margarine, melted
2 tablespoons chopped fresh parsley
Freshly ground pepper
Dash paprika

Saute the garlic in the melted butter and remove from heat. Stir in lime juice, parsley, pepper and paprika. Arrange shrimp in a hinged grilling basket (or thread on skewers) and baste liberally with the lime-butter sauce. Grill over medium-hot coals about three to five minutes, basting frequently and turning basket three times. Serves four.

# Savory Shrimp Grill

2 pounds shrimp, raw but shelled and deveined, leave tails on
2 cloves garlic, crushed
½ cup soy sauce
1 tablespoon honey
½ cup lemon juice
¼ cup chopped fresh parsley
Freshly ground black pepper

Place shrimp in a shallow glass container. Make a marinade by mixing the remaining ingredients and pour over shrimp. Refrigerate one hour. Thread shrimp on skewers and grill over medium coals, three to five minutes, basting with marinade often and turning often. Serves four.

# Grilled Scampi

2 pounds shrimp, shelled, leaving tails on
1 cup olive oil
4 cloves garlic, minced
½ cup minced onions
¼ cup lemon juice
2 tablespoons chopped fresh basil
¼ cup chopped fresh parsley
Freshly ground black pepper
Heavy duty aluminum foil for cooking

Place shrimp in a shallow glass container. Combine remaining ingredients and pour over shrimp. Refrigerate and marinate at least four hours.

Cut eight squares of aluminum foil and divide shrimp between these, sealing edges carefully. Place packets over medium coals and cook for six to eight minutes. Turn and cook another six minutes. Serves eight.

# Soups and Stews

# Seaside Stew

1 pound bacon fried crisp and crumbled
1 medium onion, chopped
1½ cups white wine
2 one-pound, 14-ounce cans tomatoes, chopped
1 four-ounce can mushrooms, drained
1 pound firm-fleshed fish like sole, cubed
½ pound shrimp, uncooked, but shelled and deveined
½ pound scallops
½ pound crab meat
2 four and a half-ounce cans chopped clams with liquid
Salt and pepper to taste
Basil

In a small amount of bacon drippings, saute the onion. Add white wine, tomatoes, mushrooms and fish. Simmer about one hour. Add shrimp, scallops, crab meat and clams. Cover and simmer about 20 minutes. Season to taste with salt, pepper and basil. Serves six to eight.

# Captain's Shrimp Chowder

2½ pounds shrimp, uncooked, shelled and deveined
6 cups water, boiling
1 small onion, chopped
3 bay leaves
1 tablespoon vinegar
4 slices bacon, chopped and fried crisp
1 green pepper, chopped
2 stalks celery, chopped
2 small onions, chopped
2 potatoes, diced
1 one-pound can tomatoes, chopped

Rinse shrimp and along with the chopped onion, bay leaves and vinegar, add to boiling water. Cook about five minutes, or until shrimp are done. Remove shrimp and set aside.

Strain water and reserve. In same pan, saute bacon and in drippings, saute the green pepper, celery and additional two onions until soft. Add diced potatoes and tomatoes with juice from can. Simmer about 20 minutes or until all vegetables are cooked. Add reserved water from cooking shrimp and bring to a boil. Add shrimp cooking just long enough to heat the shrimp.

If desired, add one tablespoon dry sherry to each soup bowl before ladeling in soup. Serves six to eight.

# Summer Shrimp Chowder

2 cups shrimp, cooked, shelled and chopped
16 ounces fresh mushrooms, washed, trimmed and sliced
1 teaspoon salt
1½ cups water
2 green onions, sliced, tops included
3 tablespoons butter or margarine
¼ cup all-purpose flour
2 cups milk
1 cup light cream
Dash each of freshly ground pepper and nutmeg

In a two-quart or larger saucepan, combine the mushrooms with the salt and water and bring to a boil. Reduce heat and cover. Simmer about 10 minutes.

In a small skillet, saute the onions in the butter. Gradually stir in the flour, stirring and cooking until smooth. Blend in the mushroom mixture, slowly, stirring and cooking until smooth and thickened. Stir in milk and then cream. Add shrimp and chill thoroughly. Dust with pepper and nutmeg before serving. Serves six.

# Pea Soup With Shrimp

3 beef bouillion cubes
3 cups hot water
½ cup chopped onion
1 large carrot, scraped and cubed
½ teaspoon each dry sage and tarragon
1 10-ounce package frozen green peas
2 cups shrimp, cooked and shelled, halved if large or
    two 4½-ounce cans shrimp, drained
½ cup light cream or undiluted evaporated milk
½ cup dry sherry
Salt and pepper to taste

Combine bouillion cubes, water, onion and carrot. Bring to a boil and cook until vegetables are tender. Add herbs and peas and bring to a boil. In a food processor or blender, process this mixture until pureed. Return to pan and add shrimp, cream, sherry and season to taste with salt and pepper. Heat through and serve. Serves four.

# Gazpacho With Shrimp

1 4½-ounce can shrimp, liquid reserved
1 cucumber, unpeeled and sliced
1 medium onion, sliced
1 green pepper, seeded and sliced
1 clove garlic
¼ cup fresh parsley
4 cups canned tomato juice
¼ teaspoon bottled hot pepper sauce
2 tablespoons olive oil
Juice of one lemon
Freshly ground black pepper

Chill shrimp, vegetables and tomato juice. In bowl of food processor or in blender, place cucumber, onion, green pepper, garlic and parsley. Process to almost pureed. Combine with tomato juice, hot pepper sauce, olive oil, lemon juice, shrimp and shrimp liquid. Serve well chilled with a dusting of black pepper. Serves four to six.

# Iceberg Shrimp Cream Soup

1 four and a half-ounce can shrimp
1 medium head iceberg lettuce, trimmed and cored
1 medium onion, sliced
2 cups water
1 tablespoon butter or margarine
2 vegetable or chicken boullion cubes
¼ cup heavy cream or undiluted evaporated milk
Salt and freshly ground pepper to taste
Dash nutmeg

Cut lettuce in fourths and place in a soup kettle with the onion and water. Cover and cook over medium-high heat about five minutes or until lettuce is wilted. Strain, reserving liquid. Add butter and boullion cubes to the liquid and set aside. Puree lettuce and onion in food processor or blender. Add the puree, cream, shrimp and liquid from can to the seasoned liquid. Season with salt and pepper to taste. Heat and serve, with a dash of nutmeg on each serving. This soup can also be chilled and served cold. Serves five.

# Easy Shrimp Bisque

¾ pound shrimp, cooked, shelled and cleaned
1 green onion, chopped, top included
2 tablespoons chopped celery
¼ cup butter or margarine
2 tablespoons all-purpose flour
¼ teaspoon paprika
Dash freshly ground pepper and dash nutmeg
4 cups whole milk
Fresh parsley, chopped for garnish, optional

Grind shrimp or chop fine and set aside. Saute onion and celery in butter. Blend in flour, paprika, pepper and nutmeg, stirring constantly until thickened and smooth. Gradually add milk, stirring until smooth and thickened slightly. Add shrimp and heat through. Garnish with parsley. Serves six.

# Sunset Bisque

2 10¾-ounce cans cream of shrimp soup
1 10¾-ounce can cream of tomato soup
3 cups whole milk
¼ cup dry sherry
1 4½-ounce can shrimp, drained and chopped
½ cup heavy cream, whipped for garnish
Freshly ground black pepper
Dash nutmeg
Chopped parsley

Combine first four ingredients, heat, stirring until smooth. Stir in chopped shrimp and heat through. Serve with a dollop of the whipped cream in each bowl. Dust whipped cream with black pepper, nutmeg and parsley. Serves six.

*Gumbos are a specialty of the Gulf Coast, especially Louisiana, and are more stews than soups. The file' powder used to thicken some gumbos is made from sassafras leaves. That southern vegetable, okra, is often an ingredient in gumbo. The name "gumbo" was derived from the African word for okra, which is also often used to thicken the stews. The following gumbo uses crab, oysters and ham in addition to shrimp.*

## Seafood-Okra Gumbo

¼ cup vegetable oil
3 pounds fresh okra, thinly sliced
⅓ cup each all-purpose flour and vegetable oil, mixed
3 cups chopped onion
1 quart water
2 tablespoons tomato paste
2 pounds raw shrimp, peeled and deveined
1 pound crab meat
1 cup ham, diced
1 pint oysters
½ cup chopped parsley
2 cloves garlic, minced
3 bay leaves
1 cup celery, chopped
Hot pepper sauce to taste
Hot cooked rice

In the one-quarter cup oil, saute the okra until soft and thickened. Set aside. In a heavy pot, cook and stir the paste made of the oil and flour, until it is thick and browned, about 20 minutes. Add onion, water and tomato paste. Stir in the okra, then the shrimp, crab, ham and oysters. Stir in parsley, garlic, bay leaves and celery. Simmer, uncovered, about one hour. Season to taste with hot pepper sauce, and serve over hot rice. Serves 12.

# Gulf Gumbo

1 pound shrimp, raw and shelled
2 medium onions, sliced
1 green pepper, chopped
2 cloves garlic, minced
½ cup butter or margarine
2 tablespoons all-purpose flour
1 eight-ounce can tomato sauce
1 10-ounce package frozen cut okra
1 15-ounce can tomatoes, chopped, liquid reserved
2 beef bouillion cubes
1½ cups hot water
2 tablespoons Worcestershire sauce
⅛ teaspoon powdered cloves
½ teaspoon dried basil leaves, crumbled
2 bay leaves
¼ teaspoon freshly ground black pepper

Saute onions, garlic and pepper in the butter. Blend in flour, stirring until smooth. Dissolve the bouillion cubes in the hot water and add to pan with vegetables. Stir until smooth. Add remaining ingredients, except shrimp and simmer stirring occasionally, about 35 minutes, covered. Add shrimp and simmer 15 minutes longer. Serve in bowls, over hot rice if desired. Serves four to six.


# Indian Summer Soup

1½ pounds shrimp, raw and shelled
¼ cup vegetable oil
2 tablespoons all-purpose flour
1 large onion, chopped
1 large green pepper, chopped
12 ears fresh corn, kernals cut from cobs and cobs scraped
½ cup tomato sauce
Water
Freshly ground black pepper

Make a roux of the flour and oil, heating and cooking to brown and thicken. Add onion and saute. Then add green pepper, corn and tomato sauce, adding enough water to desired consistency. Simmer about 30 minutes, or until vegetables are done. Add shrimp and simmer about 15 minutes more, until the shrimp are done. Season with pepper and salt if desired. Serves eight.

*Another Creole dish is jambalaya. Traditionally jambalaya is a rice dish cooked with tomatoes, seafood or poultry, onions and herbs. The dish was believed to have been introduced into the cookery of Louisiana when the Spanish controlled New Orleans. Jambalaya resembles that Spanish dish, paella. Jambalaya is frequently eaten as a stew and is served in a bowl. There are countless variations of this dish. The following is a soup which calls on ham and shrimp.*

## *Jambalaya Soup*

1 ham bone
5 cups water
2 stalks celery
1 carrot, scrubbed
1 small onion, quartered
1 pound small shrimp or two 4½-ounce cans shrimp
2 cups chopped ham
1 medium onion, chopped
2 cloves garlic, minced
1 cup chopped celery
3 tablespoons butter or margarine
¼ cup bottled chili sauce
1 eight-ounce can tomato sauce
2 cups cut okra or one 10-ounce package frozen cut okra
½ cup long grain rice
¼ teaspoon each black and red cayenne pepper

In a large pot combine the ham bone, water, two stalks of celery, carrot and quartered onion. Bring to a boil and then simmer about 45 minutes to one hour. Strain broth and discard vegetables and bone. In another pan, saute the onion, garlic and celery in the butter. Add to broth. Add ham, tomato sauce, chili sauce and rice. Bring to a boil again and then simmer, covered about 15 minutes, or until rice is done. Add okra and shrimp and cover and heat five minutes more, or until okra and shrimp are done. Season with peppers. Serves six.

# Selected Bibliography

Alvarez, J., Andrew, C.O. and Prochaska, F. *Economic Structure of the Florida Shrimp Processing Industry.* Gainesville, Fla.: Florida Sea Grant Program, 1979.

Anderson, C.O., Prochaska, F. J. and Alvarez, J. *Florida Shrimp: From the Sea Through the Market.* Gainesville, Fla.: Florida Sea Grant Program, 1975.

Bliss, D. E. *Shrimps, Lobsters and Crabs.* Piscataway, N.J.: New Century Publishers, Inc., 1982.

Caldwell, F. E. *Pot Fishing Alaskan Shrimp.* Anchorage, Alaska: Alaska Magazine, July 1979.

Donaldson, G. *Mariculture Abroad in a Dark Cloud Looming on Domestic Horizon, National Fisherman Yearbook 1985.* Camden, Maine: Journal Publications, 1985.

Gibbons, E. *Stalking the Blue-Eyed Scallop.* New York: David McKay Company, Inc., 1964.

Graham, G. *Sport Shrimp Trawling.* College Station, Texas: Center for Marine Resources, 1976.

Hardigree, P.A. *The Free Food Seafood Book.* Harrisburg, Pa.: Stackpole Books, 1978.

Headstrom, R. *All About Lobsters, Crabs, Shrimps and Their Relatives.* New York: Dover Publications, 1979.

Hertzberg, R., Vaughn, B. and Greene, J. *The New Putting Food By.* Brattlebobo, Vt.: The Stephen Greene Press, 1982.

Moore, C. J. *A Recreational Guide to Oystering, Clamming, Shrimping and*

*Crabbing in South Carolina.* Charleston, S.C.: South Carolina Wildlife and Marine Resources Department.

Morris, R. A. and Prochaska, F. *Economic Impact of the Processing and Marketing of the Commercial Florida Marine Landings.* Gainesville, Fla.: Florida Sea Grant Program, 1979.

Robinson, R. H. *Left to Your Own Devices.* Georgetown, Del.: Shellfish Series, 1982.

Walther, L. L. *Stalking the Great Stalker.* Georgetown, Del.: Shellfish Series, 1980.

Wescott, W. *Recreational Shrimping: Nets, Doors and Power.* Raleigh, N.C.: University of North Carolina Sea Grant, 1983.

# *Trap and Net Sources*

## Shrimp Traps

Friendship Trap Co., Route 97, Box 477, Friendship, ME 04547
Shrimp Traps: 36" x 24" x 15" of coated wire mesh

Gino Litrico, Post Office Box 742, Fernandina Beach, Florida 32034
"Trigger Net"

Ted Lund, net and trap maker, Banana Bay No. 2410, 200 S. Banana River Blvd., Cocoa Beach, Florida 32931
Shrimp Traps: 24" x 48" x 12" of galvanized hardware cloth

Warehouse Marine, 4714 Ballard Avenue N.W., Seattle WA 98107
Folding Shrimp Trap: 27" and 34" diameter of nylon netting and galvanized hoops

## Cast Nets

Ted Lund, net and trap maker, Banana Bay No. 2410, 200 S. Banana River Blvd., Cocoa Beach, Florida 32931
Shrimp cast and seine nets made to order

# *Index*

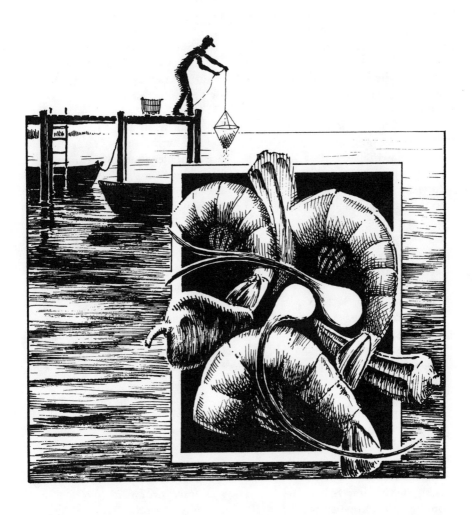

# Notes